Rangoon creeper (*Combretum indicum*) — Photo credit: Vivek Balu

GARDENING WITH NATIVE AND NATURALISED FLORA OF INDIA

Vikas Bhat & Vivek Balu

First published in 2024

ISBN – 9798339715603

Cover and Book design by Vivek Balu , with inputs from Dr. Varsha
Balu & Mr. Sanjay Balu.

CONTENTS

2

FOREWORD

In India, there are about 17,500 species of angiosperms which account for 39% of the total Indian flora (It is estimated that about 45,000 species of plants occur in India). Among the Indian species, about 10% of the entire angiospermic plants have been considered as endangered and threatened. Over 4,000 of India's angiosperm species are endemic to the country and largely concentrated in three biodiversity hotspots, viz. the Western Ghats, the Himalayas and the Indo-Burma region. As far as biodiversity point of view is concern, the Western Ghats, the Himalayas and the Indo-Burma region are the important areas in India.

The hotspots regions are under huge human pressure and numbers of species are rare, endangered and threatened (RET). The rapid depletion of natural vegetation due to natural factors and other anthropogenic activities on the fragile natural ecosystems, has caused considerable depletion in the natural populations of most endemics. In recent years, increasing loss of biodiversity has created serious threats to the survival of mankind. The main causes of biodiversity loss are habitat destruction, deforestation. pollution, population, invasive weed, over exploitation and climate change. Destruction of the habitat is the major threat of biodiversity. Therefore, it has become necessary to conserve endemic and threatened plants of hotspots regions through various garden techniques. Without knowledge of species and their correct identity, nothing can be done with reference to their conservation and utilization.

Authors have provided brief information about the types of garden in this book which include natural garden, native plants, selection of plants as per the geo climatic and agro climatic zones for maximum propagation benefits, garden basics- layout of a garden and parameters that are of prime importance i.e. air, water, sunlight, soil, temperature, nutrients. Also covered are different types of gardens, Butterfly gardens, Herbal gardens / Medicinal gardens, Water gardens / Aqua gardens, Astrology gardens, Vastu gardens, Vertical gardens, etc. and recommended with some species that are to be used and explained with different growing techniques. The main focus of this book is on the 100 native and naturalised angiospermic plant species with botanical name, common / local name, distribution, summary / short description, medicinal wheel, uses, growing tips and good photo of plant for easy to identification.

Many of the native plants have not been identified and examined. Every year around 10 new species are getting identified. Numerous native plants that have been identified have not been analyzed properly for their chemical constituents and potential uses. The alarming rate of extinction of native plants makes it impossible for conservation.

India being a nature worshiping culture, has celebrated plants as divine creations and worthy of respect and numerous verses are there from the earliest cave paintings to Vedic literature as well as puranas, itihasas, literary works through the ages right up to modern times.

The main aim of this book is to develop awareness among society about gardening with native and naturalised plants.

Dr. A. N. Chandore

Authors Note

Why the need for biodiversity gardening?

We are at the end of an epoch, and there has been a fundamental shift in the ecology in India. There is dramatic change happening in the floral biodiversity due to the increased infrastructure, diversion of land towards development and fragmentation of land

There is currently a mass extinction of our native species. Many of which hold invaluable potential medicinally, ecologically, culturally and much more.

This is because of the destruction and diversion of land use, but also because of the spread of invasive plants. These invasive plants are brought in by the gardening trade, and some who succeed manage to spread outside our gardens and overtake all our indigenous species.

They do not play a positive role in the local ecosystem and do not feed any animal or bird, which is why they continue to spread.

There is a need more than ever to document native plants in their natural habitat, because these habitats are rapidly changing, there is no record how these plants coexisted in their niche habitats.

Currently, there is a lacunae in plant community experts. We have taxonomists who are able to identify but unable to grow these plants. We have gardeners and farmers, who are able to grow these plants, but not aware of how to identify them on a scientific basis. We have landscape architects who know how to group plants to make them look appealing, but do not know how to grow or identify plants. This leaves a massive gap in the understanding of plant communities.

To understand how plant communities coexist needs a scientific but intuitive method of observation. It is a cultivation of the mind rather than the plants. In this approach to growing plants, you look at the whole system rather than one plant. Instead of just appreciating one plant's features, we look at the soil, the plants growing around it, the surrounding geoclimatic conditions and much more.

When you approach a forest with this approach, you are able to see a whole community and appreciate its interactions rather than just single plants. This gives you an ability to understand a much larger system that can be applied to gardening as well.

What can we do to save them?

We can only save our native species if the gardening community takes them into our gardens instead of just buying foreign species. This gives them a chance to reproduce and recolonize the wild spaces which they used to live in.

These plants are the plants our grandparents grew up around. By keeping them in your garden, you are not only feeding the birds and bees but also carrying forward the medicinal, culinary and cultural heritage.

Vikas Bhat

Authors Note

Welcome to our exploration of gardening with native and naturalised plants! Initially envisioned as a basic introduction, to this world of flora, this book has evolved into a more detailed resource, involving holistic aspects of gardening. As we delved deeper into the characteristics, health benefits, and vibrant personalities of these plants, we recognized the importance of presenting our findings in a clear, engaging format.

Some of the quick reference tools that are used in the book include:

· **Maps**: Our maps provide a visual overview of the species and their geographic origins, making it easier for you to select the right plants for your garden.

· **Summary Table**: This table offers a bird's-eye view of the species of flora, summarizing key attributes and uses at a glance.

· **Medicinal Wheel**: It highlights the various uses of these plants practices. Please note that the medicinal properties mentioned are based on existing studies and research; we encourage readers to consult additional resources for verification.

This publication marks our inaugural journey into exploring native and naturalised flora and we anticipate some "beginner's bloomers" along the way. We are committed to refining our content based on your feedback and new insights as we continue to learn and grow.

Thank you for joining us on this gardening adventure! Together, we can cultivate not only beautiful spaces but also inculcate a deeper appreciation for the native and naturalised plants that enrich our lives.

Vivek Balu

12

CHAPTER 1

What is a natural garden?

A natural garden is one where the gardener tries to align the garden to be in tune with the natural order of things. This can be achieved by studying nature and natural processes for ideas, methods and solutions. The effect has to be real and practical and serve the goal and purpose of the larger ecosystem, within which one's garden exists. Natural gardens have to be rich in biodiversity and contain numerous native plants species. Due to this they can serve as conservatories and propagation centers of many rare and endangered species.

The plants of a region that are naturally occurring or were occurring at one time is referred to as native species that would likely have existed had the place not been disturbed and plants that were introduced many hundreds of years ago and have ingrained and adapted itself in our eco-system are called naturalised plants.

Our garden exists on ancient lands which evolved over millions of years in conjunction with numerous animals, birds, insects and microorganisms which constitutes to the biota of the region. Gardens have existed from time immemorial in India and around the world and have been featured in Vedic manuscripts such as "Uparana Vinoda". In ancient ayurveda under the topic "Vriksh ayurveda".These texts have also stressed the significance of Soil Health, Propagation, Pest control, Significance and importance of flora and the advantages of biodiversity in nature. Herbal and healing properties of plants have been described in Ayurveda.

Gardens in ancient India to the present have always played a very significant impact on human life. From as early as 1500 BC, and in the Indian epics Mahabharata and the Ramayana it has been emphasized that gardens were part and parcel of a natural co-existence on the planet.

This book's main emphasis is about using native and naturalised species in your Garden.

In a natural garden preference is given to our beautiful native species and naturalised species as they support numerous varieties of native insects and birds and promote a rich eco-system.

There are some alarming statistics emerging about the shocking loss of insects and bird species. Many are almost gone. Our natural garden helps stop the loss and will support the reestablishment of flora and fauna. In an existing garden I would recommend a gradual transition to native species is much more suitable as and when vacancies or opportunity arise the appropriate native species can be added to the garden space.

On the other hand in a new garden the need to start from scratch offers scope to straight away plunge into natural gardening.

CHAPTER 2

Native plants

The plants have evolved over a long period of time and are designed by mother nature to be suited for that type of geoclimatic conditions in which they have evolved are native plants. Each particular niche within a geoclimatic region has plants that are adapted to occupy and and thrive where ever such niche are available.

Among native plants a few are classified as endemic plants, they have a much more restricted ranges unlike native plants which can be native to many countries and even continents. Some of these endemics have an extremely small ranges sometimes as little as few square km or a single valley. Since all life forms are interconnected and live off and coexist in an interdependent relationship. Insects, birds, microorganisms, animals of that area are all influenced and impacted by the plant species that live there.

Native flora and geoclimatic zones

India has almost all types of climatic and geographical regions. An agro climatic zone is an area that has certain common features like temperature, soil condition, weather, rainy season. India has around 15 agro-climatic zones. (Each zone has variety of flora and fauna most suited for that habitat).

We keep this in mind while choosing plants for the natural garden as India is a vast subcontinent, and thus has numerous geoclimatic regions.

India is also blessed with a few really amazing global bio diversity hotspots which are very dense in species and rich in numerous beautiful and varied flora and fauna.

Native plants are the wealth of India.

The native plants are able to support the birds and butterflies of that zone with their flowers, fruits, and conditions needed for mating and survival. Totally India has approximately 58300 registered species of plants. Among them are some of the most beautiful plants which will be excellent garden plants. Many are very useful herbs and medicinal plants having vast potential to improve human life.

Many of the native plants have not been identified and examined. Every year around 10 new species are getting identified. Numerous native plants that have been identified have not been analyzed properly for their chemical constituents and potential uses. The alarming rate of extinction of native plants makes it impossible for conservation.

They are species that can grow well, and propagate on their own without human assistance and care taking. Within each region variations are present in altitude, location, level of disturbance, water availability, soil fertility etc.

Native plants can be brought down into further categories:

1. Endemic plants.

They only occur in a particular region or part of a small section of the region. Endemic plants often have a very narrow range. Often on a specific mountain or valley, most of these are rather delicate or peculiar plants that may require specific climatic conditions, soil, rainfall etc. Almost all of the endemic plants are in great degrees of extinction.

2. Naturalised invasive plants

Some of the invasive plants have arrived long ago and naturalised in our region. These are the naturalised invasive plants. Many of these are excellent fruit or flowering trees. They were brought into in historical times by traders. Some of the important naturalised exotic plants include chikoo, breadfruit, cashew, chilli and numerous flowering plants and trees that were brought in by colonial persons from Africa, Europe, Americas and Australia.

3. Dangerous invasive weeds /plants

The second category are dangerous invasive weeds. These are usually very versatile plants that tend to have lots of seeds, self-propagate very easily and escape and multiply very fast and vigorously. They destroy the area by their presence. Competing with native species very vigorously, they usually overpower the native species and cause ecological disaster.

Newly arrived (post 1980) species that have been recklessly imported by garden trade are another group of plants many of which are steadily turning into invasive weeds after escaping from garden. The global interest in gardening has boomed as urbanization of humans increase all over the world. Also the smaller spaces we occupy like urban landscapes are devoid of natural vegetation. Nostalgia for the lost nature and the immense happiness tending to plants, provide are the main driving forces of growth of international trading of exotic plants from far of countries.

These foreign plants are evolved in very different geoclimatic zones have hardly any connection to places they end up in, like your garden or balcony. Propagated in numerous nurseries and spread out into the exotic country through gardening hobbies. Since India contains numerous geoclimatic regions from desert to alpine to tropical rain forest spread out from Himalayas to Indian ocean across some 30 states, these exotic plants eventually reach every corner through the plants and gardening trade and its networking. From private gardens and public ones for they can easily escape and start going in the ideal regions. Approximately 25% of foreign plants have arrived by unknown ways. Most of them are imported for either usefulness for agriculture or for gardening purposes.

These intentionally or accidentally imported plants are a great threat to the biodiversity of our native and endemic species. Not only native plants are threat due to the vigour and propensity of many of them when they escape and become invasive weeds. But one has to remember that local butterflies, moths, ants, birds, insects, animals all depend on our native plants for their food and every requirement.

One of the greatest dangers or threats is the extinction of bees all over the world, due to the increase in invasive, non bee friendly species and hence the pressing need to plant more native species which attract bees/ butterflies automatically. Bees help plants reproduce by spreading pollen from flower to flower. This process is called pollination, and is essential for the production of about one third of the world's food.

They are part of the biodiversity that's essential for human survival. They help maintain ecosystems and protect plant and animal species. Bees can indicate the health of environment. By observing the health of bees, we can learn about changes in the environment and take action to protect it. They produce products like honey, wax and propolis which are valuable to humans and commercially valuable. Almost 90 % of wild plants and 75 % of leading global crops depend on animal pollination. One out of every three mouthfuls of our food depend on pollinators such as bees. Crops that depend on pollination are five times more valuable than those that do not.

Invasive plants VS native plants impact

Invasive species – They displace native species, create food deserts and destroys all other species of fauna that are dependent on the native plants. So, in a nutshell foreign, alien plants are a menace to environment, quality of life and biodiversity of our region.

Selection of plants

It is recommended that you select your plants as per the Geo climatic zones and Agro climatic Zones for maximum propagation benefits.

Geo climatic zones:-

What are geo climatic zones?

They help in understanding the long term pattern of weather in a particular region.

The five major climate zones are: Tropical, dry, moderate, continental, polar

1. Tropical climates are humid and hot.
2. Dry climates receive less than 16 inches

of rainfall per year.

3. Moderate / Temperate climates are warm and humid in the summer and have mild winters.

4. Continental climates have cold winters and long lasting snow.

5. Polar climates have very cold winters, cool summers and freezing temperatures for most of the year

India has some of the world's most bio diverse eco zones—

Deserts, mountains, highlands, tropical and temperate forests, swamp lands, plains, grasslands, areas surrounding rivers and islands.

It hosts three bio diverse hotspots: the Western Ghats, the Himalayas and the Indo-Burma region.

A biodiversity hotspot is a region that has a high number of species, including many that are unique to the area. To be considered a hotspot, a region must meet two criteria:

- Endemic species: Have at least 1,500 plant species that are unique to the planet

- Threatened: Have lost at least 70% of

their native vegetation.

Agro climatic zones:-

An "Agro-climatic zone" is a land in terms of major climates, suitable for a certain range of crops. The aim is scientific management of regional resources to meet the food, fibre, fodder and fuel wood without adversely affecting the status of natural resources and environment.

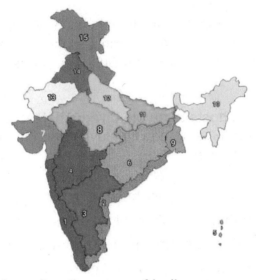

Agroclimatic zones of India

The map represents the agro climatic zones in India.

1. West coast plains and hills

2. East coast plains and hills
3. Southern plateau and hills
4. Western plateau and hills
5. Islands
6. Eastern plateau and hills
7. Gujarat plains and hills
8. Central plateau and hills
9. Lower Gangetic plain
10. Eastern Himalaya
11. Middle Gangetic plains
12. Upper Gangetic plains
13. Western dry region
14. Trans Gangetic plains
15. Western Himalaya

The plants that occur in an area naturally are directly connected or evolved to the surrounding zone, to survive. First step for us after finalizing on the place for the upcoming garden, identifying the geoclimatic zone is important, and accordingly first preference should be given to naturally occurring species of your zone. Some plants of other zones also will survive quite well, but they will often need additional support to survive. Some of the species are very versatile and hardy and can survive very well in numerous zones, particularly some of the popular traditional garden plants which are available in many nurseries.

India's rich Plant Heritage

India being a nature worshiping culture, has celebrated plants as divine creations and worthy of respect and numerous verses are there from the earliest cave paintings to Vedic literature as well as puranas, itihasas, literary works through the ages right up to modern times. Every village where Hindus live have some sacred trees and temples with gardens and attached deity trees. Numerous species are saved in thousands of sacred groves and hills, mountains, and temple gardens.

Some of the most famous temples are directly connect to a sacred tree- like, Annapurna, vanadurga etc. Almost all communities have their own sacred sites with associated trees. For every puja, havans, and festivals –flowers, sacred tree wood and twigs (*Ficus palash*) etc. are essential. For laxmi pooja lotus, for lord Shiva bilva, for lord Vishnu tulsi and every nakshatra has its own tree species.

Chapter 3

GARDEN BASICS

Now that we have left some serious stuff behind let's embark on planting our Garden. We have all heard the word "Green Thumb" apparently referring to successful gardeners who seem to have lovely lush plants, flowers, vegetable and whatever they decide to plant compared to others who similarly endeavour with less success. Well we feel the real thing that makes a "Green Thumb" is the person's passion and love for gardening.

Gardening is believed to restore and reinvigorate all the 5 senses and flowers have high healing and therapeutic effects. (Hence the practise of sending flowers to the ailing or carrying them to hospitals).

Ok let us hit the basics,

Layout of a garden:

While there is no hard and fast rule for a general garden layout some parameters are of prime importance.
Air, Water, Sunlight, Soil, Temperature, Nutrients.

Air: Plants take in carbon-dioxide from the air to make food and release oxygen in a process called "Photosynthesis" which is vital for their growth.

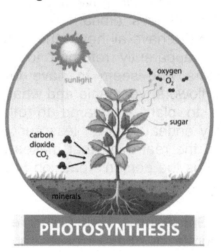

Water: The general consensus is that water is the life line of the plant and has numerous functions inside a plant it spreads nutrients to all parts of the plant, it helps in photosynthesis and regulates the temperature of the plant.

The issue here is that every plant has a different level of water requirement and to achieve this a small study is necessary.

Too much water tends to clog the roots, block air pockets and hamper air flow resulting in damage to the plant cells and lack of water will result in the plant perishing so its paramount to keep the beds wet and moist all the time that is to increase watering in summer, less in colder times and water only if needed during rainy seasons.

Sunlight: As in most creation sunlight is vital to the growth of you garden, the most commonly talked about types are ,

1. Bright sunlight
2. Partial Sunlight
3. Diffused Sunlight

Sunlight plays a part in photosynthesis and in the general well being of the plant. The issue here is different plants need varying degrees of sunlight and the common symptom you can notice if the light is too much leaves turn pale brown and burn and if it is too little there is yellowing of the leaves and as such suitable remedial measures should be taken.

Soil: Since there are different types of soils, like red, black soils we need to check the regions of our garden as soils are unique to regions. The best way is to see what kind of soil is available at your location and enhance it in the best possible ways. As most soils are a mixture of the above mentioned grey /black and red soils along with clay content the following measures are recommended.

Addition of manure in needed measures
Addition of Compost and Vermi compost
Addition of coco peat

Removal of all waste substances in the soil like impurities, rocks, stones and other foreign materials. As you start the process and gain experience you will comprehend which mixtures are best suited in the basic soil available to you.

Temperature: Plants basically thrive between temperatures of 15 to 35 degrees centigrade and there are species that thrive in extremities as well. Temperatures are divided into three sections High, medium and Low. High temperatures are usually above 35 degrees centigrade and are suitable for hydrophobic tropical plants that adapt to arid conditions.
Some examples are *Nerium oleander*, Cacti and *Tamarindus indica*.

Medium temperatures are usually between

15 to 35 degrees centigrade and are typical tropical foliage plants. Most of the plants thrive in this temperature.

Low Temperatures are between 0 and 15 degrees centigrade and are borne by winter loving plants
Ex: Calendula and Marigold.

Nutrients: The most common nutrients used in the market are called NPK
(Nitrogen, potassium and Phosphorus).The Nutrients a plant needs are Carbon, nitrogen, Oxygen, Phosphorus and potassium.While the nutrients as a whole play a huge part in the development of the plant, individually each of them contribute in specific ways,

Carbon:
Increases water storage capacity and prevents erosion
Nitrogen:
Lack of it will result in stunted growth and discolouration of leaves.
Oxygen:
Aids in respiration and carrying nutrients to all the plant cells.
Potassium:
Lack of it, results in issues with propagation and reproduction and discolouration of leaves.
Phosphorus:

Lack of it makes the plant weak and immune to all types of threats.

Apart from the Chemical nutrients and fertilizers the demand for organic natural fertilizers is huge. Organic fertilizers comprising of Manure or Compost is the natural option. Compost is made up of food waste and Manure is made from the excreta of cattle. Depending on the size of the garden a suitable mix of both these nutrients will yield the desired results.

CHAPTER 4

Different Types of gardens

Using native species, a variety of intriguing gardens can be developed. Here are some examples:

1. Butterfly Gardens
2. Herbal gardens / Medicinal gardens
3. Water gardens / Aqua gardens
4. Astrology Gardens
5. Vastu Gardens
6. Vertical Gardens

Let's take a closer look at each type of garden.

1. Butterfly Garden

Creating a butterfly garden involves understanding the life cycle of butterflies, which consists of four stages: egg, caterpillar (larva), pupa (chrysalis), and adult butterfly. Each butterfly species lays its eggs on specific plants known as larval host plants. These plants are crucial because the caterpillars that emerge from the eggs feed voraciously on their leaves. After a series of moults, the caterpillars stop eating, entering the pupal stage, where they undergo metamorphosis. After several days, the adult butterfly emerges, ready to continue the cycle.

To design an effective butterfly garden, it's essential to include a variety of native plants that serve as larval hosts for different butterfly species. Additionally, nectar-rich flowers should be planted to attract adult butterflies, ensuring a vibrant and thriving ecosystem.

Strictly avoid the use of any insecticide, pesticide, weedicide or any similar chemicals to kill pests. These will eventually kill the butterfly caterpillars and drive the butterflies away from your butterfly garden.

Some species that are recommended to be used are

1. *Ascelpias curassavica* (Tropical milkweed)

A vital larval host for monarch caterpillars, this plant attracts adult butterflies with its vibrant flowers.

2. *Buddleja asiatica* (Asiatic Butterfly Bush)

Known for its fragrant blooms, it serves as an excellent nectar source for adult butterflies.

3. *Cassia fistula* (Golden shower)

This tree produces attractive yellow flowers that are favored by various butterfly species.

4. *Cheilocostus speciosus*

With its striking flowers, it attracts butterflies while providing nectar.

5. *Crotalaria retusa*

This plant is a larval host for several butterfly species, making it essential for their life cycle.

6. *Nerium oleander* (Oleander)

While beautiful, it's important to use this plant cautiously as it's toxic; however, it can attract some butterfly species.

By incorporating these plants into your butterfly garden, you can create a sanctuary that supports both caterpillars and adult butterflies, fostering a vibrant ecosystem. Always remember to prioritize natural gardening practices to ensure the health of your garden inhabitants.

Butterfly gardens

Butterfly gardens

2. Herbal Gardens / Medicinal Gardens

An herbal or medicinal garden is a dedicated space where herbs and medicinal plants are cultivated. These gardens can be thoughtfully designed or arranged as informal patches, offering a diverse array of plants from several key families:

- **Apiaceae**: Includes plants like parsley, coriander, cumin, fennel, celery, dill, angelica, and caraway.
- **Lamiaceae**: Features aromatic herbs such as mint, basil, rosemary, sage, and thyme.
- **Alliaceae**: Comprises plants like onions, shallots, chives, and garlic.

Herbal gardens can serve many purposes, including:

Education

Herbal gardens provide valuable opportunities for learning about the cultivation, harvesting, and propagation of medicinal plants. Visitors can explore the medicinal properties of various herbs, including their scientific names, origins, and uses. This educational aspect fosters a deeper understanding of the relationship between plants and human health.

Research

These gardens can serve as important genetic resource collections, preserving vital herb varieties and their unique traits for future generations.

Health

Herbal gardens promote health by providing access to raw materials for medicinal remedies. They can also enhance local medical tourism. For instance, herbs like Thai basil are commonly used in traditional remedies, while valerian is valued for its calming effects and is often made into a soothing tea for sleep.

Culinary Use

Many herbs grown in these gardens are also used in cooking, enriching meals with fresh flavors and health benefits.

Therapeutic Benefits

The act of gardening itself can be therapeutic, providing mental and physical health benefits to those who cultivate and tend to these spaces.

By incorporating a variety of herbs, an herbal garden can serve as a multifunctional space that nurtures both the body and mind while enhancing knowledge about the natural world.

Some species that are recommended to be used are

1. *Ocimum basilicum* (Basil)

A versatile herb used in culinary dishes and known for its antimicrobial properties.

2. *Piper longum* (Long pepper)

Recognized for its medicinal uses and culinary flavor, often used in traditional medicine.

3. *Aloe vera*

Renowned for its healing properties, particularly for skin care and digestion.

4. *Coleus ambonicus* (Oregano)

Used in cooking and valued for its potential health benefits.

5. *Hibiscus rosa sinensis* (White hibiscus)

Often used in traditional remedies and teas, known for its antioxidant properties.

6. *Murraya koenigii*

Valued for its flavor in cooking and its health benefits, including digestive support.

By incorporating these plants into an herbal garden, you can create a rich environment that serves multiple purposes, from education and research to health promotion and culinary enhancement.

Herbal garden

Medicinal garden

3. Aqua Gardens

Aqua gardens are specially designed and nurtured in water bodies, focusing on growing plants that thrive in aquatic environments, particularly in the shallow margins of lakes, rivers, and ponds. While water gardens can vary in size and depth, they are often small and relatively shallow, providing a serene and visually appealing element to any landscape. Although water gardens can be almost any size or depth, they are often small and relatively shallow.

Benefits of Aqua Gardens

- **Design Element**: Water adds coolness, sparkle, and serenity to gardens. It enhances the visual appeal of landscapes, creating a tranquil environment.
- **Biodiversity**: Incorporating native fish species not only enhances the beauty of aqua gardens but also supports the ecological balance, contributing to a healthier ecosystem.
- **Recreation**: Water gardens provide opportunities for recreational activities such as fishing, swimming, or simply enjoying the tranquility of water.

- **Wildlife Habitat**: They offer habitats for various aquatic plants and animals, promoting biodiversity.

Addition of native fish species makes the aqua garden better and enhances its appeal apart from all the other benefits fish provide.

Some species that are recommended to be used are

1. *Nelumbo nucifera* (Lotus)

This iconic aquatic plant produces stunning flowers and large leaves, providing beauty and shade in the water.

2. *Zephyranthes (*Rain lily)

Known for its delicate blooms, it adds charm to the garden while thriving in wet conditions.

3. *Caltha Palustris* (Marsh marigold)

A vibrant yellow flowering plant that thrives in wet environments, bringing color to the garden.

4. Canna lilies

These bold plants feature large leaves and

striking flowers, making them a favorite in water gardens.

5. *Iris ensata*

This elegant aquatic plant produces beautiful flowers and thrives in shallow water.

6. *Crinum pedunculatum (*Coastal crinum)

Adaptable to wet conditions, this plant adds texture and interest with its large leaves and fragrant flowers.

By incorporating these plants into an aqua garden, you can create a captivating ecosystem that enhances the beauty of your landscape while supporting wildlife and providing recreational opportunities.

Aqua garden

Aqua garden

4. Astrology Gardens

Astrology gardens, also known as zodiac gardens, involve planting and growing flowers and plants according to your zodiac signs. This approach to gardening offers a unique way of self-discovery and reflects one's personality traits associated with each sign. You don't need to be a firm believer in astrology to enjoy this creative gardening style;

The idea of an astrological garden aligns plants with the energies of the zodiac signs. The practice of agro-astrology, which synchronizes sowing and harvesting with the phases of the moon, has been embraced for centuries.

Tips for Creating an Astrological Garden

1. Sow During the Waxing Moon:

Plant seeds when the moon is waxing (growing), which is believed to enhance growth and vitality.

2. Transplant in the Waning Moon:

Transplanting should be done during the waning moon (when the moon's light is decreasing).

Choose Plants Based on Your Sign:

Research which plants align with your zodiac sign and incorporate them into your garden. For example:

Taurus: Enjoys durable and fragrant flowers like roses.

Cancer: Attracted to nurturing plants like ferns

Virgo: Prefers practical herbs such as thyme and basil.

Libra: Drawn to beautiful, harmonious flowers like jasmine and lotus.

Scorpio: Interested in deep, bold colors like dark red roses.

Capricorn: Favors sturdy, enduring plants like evergreens.

Pisces: Attracted to whimsical and ethereal flowers like water lilies or lavender.

3. **Consider Planetary Influences**:

Take into account the days and times corresponding to the planets associated with your sign. For example, if your sign is ruled by Venus, consider planting on days associated with Venus for enhanced beauty and growth.

4. Create Zones in Your Garden:

Designate areas of your garden for each zodiac sign, allowing for a diverse array of plants that reflect the characteristics and energies of the signs.

Correspondence Between Plants and Zodiac Signs

Zodiac signs	Plants
Aries	Ashwaganda, Ginger
Taurus	Tulsi (Holy Basil), Cinnamon
Gemini	Brahmi, Pepper mint
Cancer	Asparagus, Lemon Balm
Leo	Coriander, Saffron
Virgo	Fennel, Tulsi (Holy Basil)
Libra	Lavender, Rose
Scorpio	Gingseng, Tulsi (Holy Basil)
Sagittarius	Ginger, Turmeric
Capricorn	Moringa, Brahmi
Aquarius	Cardamom, Tulsi (Holy Basil)
Pisces	Chamomile, Lavender

Gardening Tips for Aries

Garden Theme: Dynamic Challenge Garden

Color Palette: Red and reddish-pink

Vibrant Flowers: Geraniums and zinnias.

Accent Plants: Hibiscus.

Aries individuals are known for their boldness, energy, and willingness to take risks.

Choose striking colours: Use an abundance of red and reddish-pink flowers.

Design for adventure: Create interesting pathways or raised beds that invite exploration and engagement.

Add elements of competition: Consider a small garden area dedicated to growing vegetables or flowers.

Aries garden

Gardening Tips for Taurus

Fragrant Edibles: Lavender, hibiscus.

Leafy Herbs: Lemon balm, mint, basil.

Taureans are deeply connected to nature and enjoy sensory experiences. They appreciate fragrant plants that can enrich their surroundings, with green being their favored color.

Use Earthy Decor: Consider incorporating natural materials like stone and wood to enhance the connection with nature.

Taurus garden

Gardening Tips for Gemini

Flowers: Yellow roses.

Geminis are ruled by Mercury, the planet of communication. Their gardens thrive with vibrant, cheerful plants that reflect their lively spirit. Yellow roses are particularly favored.

Dynamic Plant Choices: Choose fast-growing herbs and plants that can be easily changed or rearranged to keep the garden fresh and engaging.

Gemini garden

Gardening Tips for Cancer

Night-Blooming flowers Jasmine, evening primrose and others like White roses, white lilies and white hibiscus.

Cancers are known for their nurturing and sensitive nature, ruled by the moon, A Cancer's garden can be filled with soft, white flowers that bloom at night.

Focus on white and light colours: Incorporate a variety of white flowers to reflect the moonlight.

Incorporate reflective elements: Add water features or mirrors to reflect the moonlight and enhance the ethereal quality of the garden.

Create a scented experience: Include fragrant herbs like mint, chamomile, and lavender which promote relaxation.

Cancer garden

Gardening Tips for Leo

Garden Theme: Perfume Garden

Colors: Orange and gold

Scented Blossoms: Orange freesia, yellow roses, marigolds and sunflowers.

Leos are vibrant, bold personalities who thrive in the limelight, radiating warmth and confidence. A perfume garden for Leo should be full of bright, sun-inspired colors and fragrant blooms .

Choose bright colour: Incorporate orange, gold, and yellow flowers.

Focus on fragrance: Select plants known for their strong scents, such as orange freesia and yellow roses, to create an inviting atmosphere.

Incorporate sun loving plants: Choose sunflowers, marigolds, and other plants that thrive in full sun to symbolize Leo's connection to the sun and its energy.

Leo garden

Gardening Tips for Virgo

Garden Theme: Medicinal and Healing

Garden

Focus: Health and Home Remedies

Medicinal Herbs: Lavender, chamomile, peppermint and aloe vera. Known for their practicality and helpful nature, Virgos excel at nurturing and supporting others. Their gardens often reflect a commitment to health and well-being, filled with medicinal plants that can be used for home remedies.

Select medicinal plants: Incorporate a variety of herbs that can be used for healing, such as lavender for relaxation and peppermint for digestion.

Include useful plants: Focus on herbs that have culinary and medicinal benefits, making your garden both beautiful and functional.

Virgo garden

Gardening Tips for Libra

Garden Theme: Harmonious Garden

Color Palette: Pink and soft pastels

Flowers: Pink roses and orchids.

Elemental Features: Incorporate stones, fountains, and small water bodies for balance. Libras are known for their appreciation of beauty, balance, and harmony.

Incorporate pink flowers: Focus on a variety of pink flowering plants like roses to create a visually harmonious and romantic setting.

Design for balance: Arrange plants and features symmetrically to promote a sense of equilibrium.

Add water features: Incorporate fountains or small water bodies to enhance the calming effect of the garden, as water represents tranquility and balance.

Libra Garden

Gardening Tips for Scorpio

Garden Theme: Mysterious Black Garden

Color Palette: Black and deep red

Dark-Foliaged Plants: Purple heart, *Acalypha wilkesiana*

Accents: Include red flowers for contrast, such as red roses or dahlias.

Scorpios are known for their depth, intensity, and sense of mystery. A black garden is a perfect reflection of their enigmatic nature.

Embrace dark colour: Use plants with deep purple, black, or dark green foliage to establish a mysterious atmosphere.

Incorporate bold reds: Introduce red flowers to create striking contrasts that reflect

Scorpio garden

Gardening Tips for Sagittarius

Garden Theme: Free-Spirited Tropical Garden

Color Palette: Blue and vibrant tropical hues

Tropical Flowers: Bougainvillea, hibiscus, and bird of paradise.

Sagittarians are adventurous and free-spirited, thriving in lively and colorful environments. A tropical garden filled with vibrant flowers and blue accents reflects their love for exploration and joy.

Gardening Tips for Sagittarius

Incorporate Tropical Blooms: Use bright and bold tropical flowers like bougainvillea and hibiscus to bring energy and vibrancy to the garden.

Use diverse textures: Combine various leaf shapes and plant heights to add interest and dynamism to the garden.

Sagittarius garden

Gardening Tips for Capricorn

Garden Theme: Practical Earthy Garden

Color Palette: Brown and earthy tones

Foliage: Evergreen shrubs, ferns and hardy perennials.

Herbs: Rosemary, thyme

Capricorns are practical, grounded, and sensible, thriving in environments that reflect their earthy nature.

Incorporate natural materials: Use wooden elements such as benches, logs, and rustic garden furniture with focus on earthy colours.

Incorporate functional elements: Consider adding raised garden beds for herbs and vegetables, aligning with Capricorn's practical side and love for functionality.

Capricorn garden

Gardening Tips for Aquarius

Garden Theme: Colorful Butterfly Garden

Color Palette: Icy blues and silvers

Butterfly-Attracting Flowers: Milkweed

and butterfly bush.

Aquarians are passionate and innovative, often drawn to ideas that promote environmental sustainability. A butterfly garden is ideal.

Choose colourful flowers: Incorporate a variety of butterfly-attracting plants that provide nectar, such as Lantana, Marigold and Buddleja.

Design for wildife: Include features that support local wildlife, such as water sources or natural shelters.

Promote Sustainability: Consider using native plants and organic gardening practices to support the environment and promote biodiversity.

Aquarius garden

Gardening Tips for Pisces

Garden Theme: Serene Water Garden

Color Palette: Soft blues and greens

Natural Water Body: A pond or stream with native aquatic plants.

Edging Plants: Wildflowers and soft grasses along the water's edge.

Pisces, as an intuitive water sign, thrive in serene and calming environments.

Incorporate a water feature: Create a natural pond or stream that serves as a focal point and habitat for native fish and aquatic plants.

Use Native aquatic plants: Select plants

like water lilies and native rushes to enhance the beauty and ecological balance of the water body.

Focus on intuition and flow:Allow the layout to flow naturally, incorporating curves and organic shapes to resonate with Pisces intuitive nature.

Pisces garden

5. Vastu gardens

Vastu Shastra, the ancient Indian science of architecture and design, emphasizes harmony and balance in living spaces, including gardens.

Overview of Do's and Don'ts of Vastu Gardens

Vastu garden do's:

1. Location:

North and East: Position the garden in the northern or eastern parts of your property to harness positive energy from the rising sun.

Water Bodies: If including a water feature, place it in the northeast corner to attract prosperity.

2. Plant Selection:

Positive Plants: Incorporate plants with positive energy, such as mango, banana, and coconut trees.

Herbs and Medicinal Plants: Grow healing herbs like tulsi (holy basil) and neem, which promote health and well-being.

3. **Garden Layout:**

Balanced Design: Ensure a balanced layout, avoiding sharp angles or chaotic arrangements. Curved pathways promote a soothing atmosphere.

Seating Areas: Create cozy seating areas in the northwest or southwest corners for relaxation and socializing.

4. **Soil Quality:**

Healthy Soil: Use fertile, healthy soil to promote robust plant growth, contributing to a vibrant energy flow.

5. **Natural Elements:**

Incorporate Natural Materials: Use natural stones, wood, and other organic materials in garden design to maintain harmony with nature.

Vastu garden don'ts:

1. **Avoid Thorny Plants:**

Stay away from thorny plants, as they are believed to create negative energy and conflict.

2. **No Dead Plants**:

Remove any dead or dying plants, as they can attract negative energy and affect the overall vibe of the garden.

3. **Limit Artificial Structures**:

Minimize the use of artificial materials like plastic, which can disrupt the natural flow of energy.

4. **Steer Clear of Chaos**:

Avoid overcrowding with too many plants or chaotic layouts, as this can create confusion and unrest in the energy flow.

5. **No Dark or Stagnant Areas**:

Ensure that all areas of the garden receive sunlight and air circulation to prevent stagnation and negativity.

Additional gardening tips for a Vastu Garden

1. **Incorporate Color**:

Use vibrant, uplifting colors in flower choices to enhance positivity and joy in the garden.

2. **Create Pathways**:

Design gentle pathways to guide visitors through the garden, promoting exploration and tranquility.

3. **Include Water Features**:

Add a small pond or fountain to encourage peaceful energy flow and attract beneficial elements.

4. **Mindful Placement**:

Carefully consider the placement of plants and features in relation to the cardinal directions for maximum positive impact.

5. **Regular Maintenance**:

Keep the garden tidy and well-maintained to ensure a positive environment and energy flow.

By following these Vastu principles and tips, you can create a harmonious garden that not only enhances your home but also promotes well-being and tranquility for all who visit.

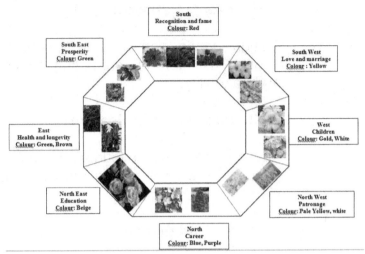

Diagram of a vastu garden

Illustration: Vivek Balu

Detailed vastu guidelines for garden design by direction

North

Do's:

1. **Location**: This location in the northern part of your property attracts positive energy.
2. **Basil Plant**: Plant a Holy Basil (Tulsi) in this area; it's considered highly auspicious.
3. **Plant Selection**: Use smaller shrubs

and plants, avoiding cacti and thorny varieties except for roses.

4. **Water Features**: Incorporate water fountains and swings to enhance relaxation and joy.
5. **Sitting Area**: Create an open sitting area with pots on the ground for comfortable gatherings.

Don'ts:

- **Avoid Large Trees**: Steer clear of huge trees that may block sunlight and energy flow.
- **No Messy Crowding**: Avoid overcrowding with plants, and refrain from using large stones or rocks.

South

Do's:

1. **Tree Planting**: This area is suitable for planting trees, providing shade and stability.
2. **Rock Gardens**: Include rock gardens and stone features for added texture and aesthetic appeal.
3. **Limited Open Space**: Keep the open space smaller to create a more intimate environment.

Don'ts:

- **No Water Bodies**: Avoid including any water features, such as pools or ponds, which can disrupt energy.
- **Avoid Crowding**: Refrain from overcrowding this area and from incorporating swings or kennels.

East

Do's:

1. **Location**: Positioning a garden in the east is beneficial, as it captures the morning sunlight.
2. **Basil Plant**: Plant Basil (Tulsi) in this area for its spiritual and health benefits.
3. **Plant Selection**: Combine small shrubs and plants with fruit-bearing trees to create a diverse and productive garden.
4. **Add Features**: Incorporate swings, fountains, and decorative pots to enhance enjoyment and relaxation.
5. **Seating**: Include seats and benches to encourage socializing and enjoying the garden space.

Don'ts:

- **Avoid Large Trees**: Steer clear of huge trees that may block sunlight.
- **No Messy Crowding**: Refrain from overcrowding the space with too many plants or heavy objects.
- **No Rock/Stone Work**: Avoid using heavy stone features that could disrupt energy flow.

West

Do's:

1. **Tree Planting**: Plant larger trees here to provide shade and a sense of enclosure.
2. **Water Bodies**: Include water features, such as ponds or fountains, to enhance the beauty and tranquility of the garden.
3. **Heavy Features**: Incorporate heavy statues and rock gardens for visual interest and stability.

Don'ts:

1. **No Crowding**: Avoid overcrowding this area, as it can create a chaotic atmosphere.
2. **No Swings or Kennels**: Refrain from including swings or kennels, which can disrupt the serenity of the space.

North-East

Do's:

1. **Water Features**: This area is ideal for pools and other water bodies, promoting positive energy and tranquility.
2. **Basil Plant**: Plant a Basil (Tulsi) and consider placing flower pots on the ground for beauty and spirituality.

Don'ts:

- **Avoid Large Trees**: Steer clear of huge trees that may block light and energy.
- **No Thorny Plants**: Refrain from using thorny plants, which can create negative energy.
- **No Crowding**: Avoid overcrowding with plants and heavy objects to maintain a serene atmosphere

North-West

Do's:

1. **Play Area**: This is a great spot for a play area, encouraging joy and activity.
2. **Water Fountain**: It's the second-best

location for a water fountain, adding a lively element to the garden.

3. **Kennels and Cages**: Ideal for placing kennels and pet cages, ensuring a designated space for pets.
4. **Cross-Pollination Plants**: Include plants that promote cross-pollination for a healthier garden ecosystem.

Don'ts:

- **No Crowding**: Avoid overcrowding this area to keep the space open and inviting.
- **No Heavy Objects**: Refrain from using heavy features that could overwhelm the garden's energy

South - East

Do's:

1. **Rose Plants**: This area is ideal for cultivating rose plants, which add beauty and positive energy.
2. **Heat-Loving Plants**: Grow plants that thrive in high temperatures, taking advantage of the sunlight in this direction.

Don'ts:

- **No Water Bodies**: Avoid any pools or water features, as they can disrupt the garden's energy.
- **No Crowding**: Steer clear of overcrowding with plants to maintain a harmonious and open space.

South-West

Do's:

1. **Tall Trees**: Planting tall trees is beneficial for providing stability and shade.
2. **Rock Gardens**: Incorporate rock gardens and heavier objects to create a grounded, solid aesthetic.
3. **Ideal Plants**: Use jasmine, roses, and marigolds, which thrive well in this area and enhance the garden's fragrance and color.
4. **Limited Open Space**: Maintain a smaller open area to foster a sense of security and enclosure.

Don'ts:

- **No Water Bodies**: Avoid including any pools or water features in this section.
- **No Crowding**: Refrain from overcrowding the space and from

placing lightweight items that can create instability.

Centre

- **Keep It Open and Clean**: The center of the garden should remain uncluttered and open to promote positive energy flow throughout the space.

Plants to avoid

According to Vastu Shastra, certain plants are considered inauspicious for gardens due to their perceived negative effects on energy and well-being:

1. **Thorny Plants**: Cacti and other thorny plants are thought to create stress and hinder relationships.
2. **Bonsai Plants**: These miniature trees are seen as representations of stunted growth.
3. **Bamboo**: Despite its popularity in some cultures, bamboo is associated with death and misfortune in Vastu.
4. **Tamarind Tree**: This tree is believed to hinder family growth and bring illness.
5. **Banyan Tree**: Its vast roots can

symbolize a heavy energy, which may not be conducive to a harmonious living environment.

6. **Creepers Indoors**: Avoid growing creepers inside the house as they can create cluttered energy.

Recommended Practices for Plants:

1. **Holy Basil (Tulsi)**: Always keep a healthy Tulsi plant inside the house for its spiritual and health benefits.
2. **Jasmine**: Planting jasmine along pathways is considered auspicious and enhances the beauty and energy of the area.
3. **Creepers**: If you choose to grow creepers in your garden, ensure they have their own support systems to thrive without damaging structures.
4. **Garden Maintenance**: Maintain a clean, well-kept, and tranquil garden to promote positive energy.

6.Vertical gardens

Vertical gardens have a rich history, with roots tracing back to ancient civilizations like the Hanging Gardens of Babylon, one of the Seven Wonders of the Ancient World. This concept has evolved over centuries, adapting to modern techniques and materials. Another notable example is the Musee Du Quai Branly Greenwall in Paris highlighting the enduring beauty and functionality of vertical gardens, merging art with nature.

In contemporary times, vertical gardening has become increasingly popular, especially in urban areas where space is limited. This innovative gardening method allows for the utilization of walls and roofs, transforming confined spaces into lush, green environments.

Vertical garden designs often prioritize eco-friendly materials and incorporate efficient irrigation systems, such as drip irrigation or hydroponics. These systems not only conserve water but also reduce waste, making vertical gardens an environmentally friendly choice.

Advantages of vertical garden

1. **Space Maximization**: Vertical gardens make the most of limited space, turning walls and other structures into vibrant green spaces.
2. **Aesthetic Appeal**: They enhance the beauty of urban landscapes, adding a touch of nature to concrete surroundings.
3. **Air Quality Improvement**: Plants in vertical gardens can help improve air quality by filtering pollutants.
4. **Temperature Regulation**: Green walls can help insulate buildings, reducing energy costs and improving indoor temperatures.

Disadvantages of Vertical Garden

While vertical gardening offers many benefits, there are also some challenges to consider:

1. **High Initial Costs**: Setting up a vertical garden can require significant investment in materials, structures, and equipment, making it less accessible for some.
2. **Special Equipment Needs**: The need for specialized systems like hydroponics or aeroponics can increase complexity and maintenance.

3. **Plant Selection**: Typically, plants suited for indoor or shade environments, such as ferns and orchids, are used, which may limit choices for those seeking a wider variety of plants.

Growing Techniques

Vertical gardening employs various techniques to optimize space and light:

1. **Terracing**: This involves creating stepped areas on hilly terrain to facilitate sustainable farming and maximize usable planting space.
2. **Trellising**: In this method, plants are secured to upright stakes using ties, allowing for upward growth and efficient use of vertical space.
3. **Tumbling**: This refers to plants that grow downwards from hanging pots, creating a cascading effect and making the most of vertical surfaces.

Examples of Vertical Garden Ideas

There are numerous creative approaches to designing vertical gardens:

- **Classic Wall Garden**: A simple arrangement of plants on a vertical surface, often using a grid or panel system.

- **Hanging Plants**: Utilizing various containers to hang plants, adding greenery without occupying ground space.
- **Wall Art**: Integrating plants into a mural or artistic design, blending nature with aesthetics.
- **Herb and Medicinal Walls**: Dedicated spaces for growing herbs and medicinal plants, easily accessible for culinary or health purposes.
- **Vegetable Shelves**: Stacked shelves or modules designed for growing vegetables vertically.
- **Moss Walls**: Using moss as a decorative element, providing a lush, green texture.

Although vertical gardening can involve higher initial costs and specialized requirements, their innovative techniques and creative designs offer a unique way to bring greenery into urban spaces.

Vertical garden in the Bengaluru
International Airport

Aegle marmelos Correa (Bael)

Aegle marmelos Correa is commonly known as bael, golden apple, stone apple or wood apple.

DISTRIBUTION

■ Native
■ Naturalised

It is native to the Indian subcontinent and Southeast Asia, Pakistan, Bangladesh, Sri Lanka, Myanmar, Thailand and Nepal.

Aegle marmelos Correa (Bael)

SUMMARY

Common Name	Bael / Wood Apple
Height	Up to 40 feet
Flower	Light Green colour
Light	Bright Sun
Origin	Indian subcontinent
Scientific name	*Aegle marmelos* Correa
Family	Rutaceae

MEDICINAL WHEEL

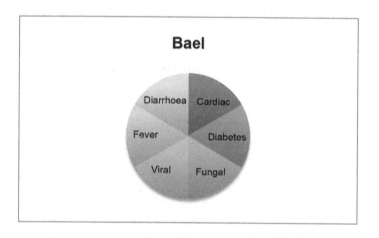

Also used as an astringent food, treat ulcers.

GROWING TIPS

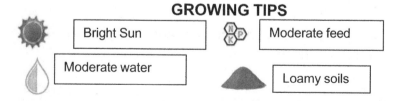

	Bright Sun		Moderate feed
	Moderate water		Loamy soils

Alangium salvifolium (Sage leaf)

Alangium salviifolium is commonly called as Sage Leaf Alangium is a tall thorny tree.

DISTRIBUTION

■ Native
■ Naturalised

It is native to Indian subcontinent and Eastern tropical Africa.

Alangium salvifolium (Sage leaf)

SUMMARY

Common	Sage Leaf Alangium/ Stone mango/ Hill sack
Height	Up to 25 feet
Flower	White to cream coloured
Light	Bright Sun
Origin	Indian subcontinent and Eastern tropical
Scientific	*Alangium salviifolium*
Family	Cornaceae

MEDICINAL WHEEL

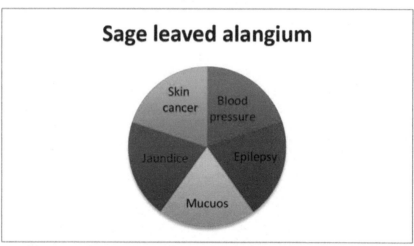

Sage leaved alangium

Skin cancer · Blood pressure · Epilepsy · Mucuos · Jaundice

Also used to cure scabies, hepatitis, diabetes etc.

GROWING TIPS

 Bright Sun

 Moderate feed

 Moderate water

 Loamy soils

Allium cepa (Onion)

Onion is a herbaceous biennial plant in the amaryllis family (Amaryllidaceae) grown for its edible bulb.

DISTRIBUTION

■ Native
■ Naturalised

It is native to Central Asia, Iran or west Pakistan. It is naturalised in India.

Allium cepa (Onion)

SUMMARY

Common Name	Onion
Height	Up to 1.5 feet
Flower	White
Light	Bright Sun
Origin	Central Asia
Scientific name	*Allium cepa*
Family	Amaryllidaceae

MEDICINAL WHEEL

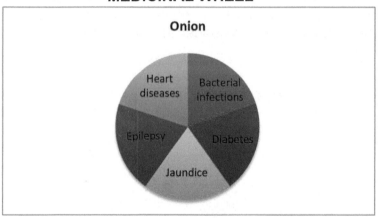

Also used to strengthens bones, treats toothache, cough, baldness, rashes etc.

GROWING TIPS

 Bright Sun   Moderate feed

 Moderate water   Loamy soils

Aloe barbadensis miller (Aloe vera)

Aloe barbadensis miller commonly called aloe vera is an evergreen perennial plant.

DISTRIBUTION

■ Native
■ Naturalised

They are native to sub-Saharan Africa, the Saudi Arabian Peninsula and to many islands of the western Indian Ocean, including Madagascar. They are naturalised in parts of China, India and United states.

Aloe barbadensis miller (Aloe vera)

SUMMARY

Common Name	Aloe vera
Height	Up to 2.5 feet
Flower	Yellow / Orange / Pink colour
Light	Bright Sun
Origin	African subcontinent
Scientific name	*Aloe barbadensis* Miller
Family	Liliaceae

MEDICINAL WHEEL

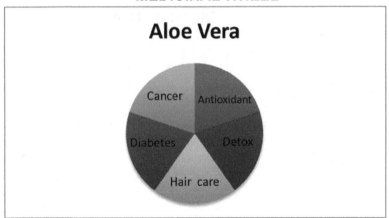

Also used to treat , psoriasis, Gastro-oesophageal Reflux Disease (GERD) etc

GROWING TIPS

 Bright Sun   Low feed

 Moderate water    Red, Loamy soils

Ananas cosmosus (Pineapple)

The *Ananas comosus* commonly known as pineapple is a tropical plant with an edible fruit, it is a significant plant in the family Bromeliaceae.

DISTRIBUTION

It is native to tropical South America, northern Argentina and Paraguay. It is naturalised in the tropical Asia.

Ananas cosmosus (Pineapple)

SUMMARY

Common Name	Pineapple
Height	Up to 4 feet
Flower	Lavender, Purple colour or Red
Light	Bright Sun
Origin	South America
Scientific name	*Ananas comosus*
Family	Bromeliaceae

MEDICINAL WHEEL

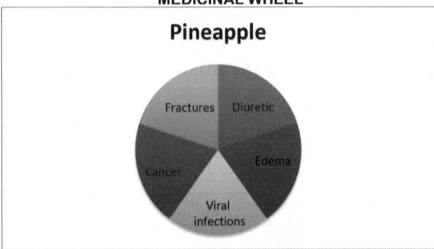

Also treat inflammations, strengthen bones, acts as diuretic and expels intestinal worms.

GROWING TIPS

 Bright Sun

 High feed

 Moderate water

 Loamy soils

Andrographis paniculata (Kalmegh)

Kalmegh is a plant which is also known as "Green Chireta" and the "King of Bitters". It is used for various medicinal purposes and is bitter in taste.

DISTRIBUTION

■ Native
■ Naturalised

It is native to the India and Sri Lanka. It is naturalised in Indonesia, Malaysia and America.

Andrographis paniculata (Kalmegh)

SUMMARY

Common Name	Green Chireta/ King of bitters
Height	Up to 1.5 feet
Flower	Purple and white colour
Light	Bright Sun
Origin	India, Sri Lanka
Scientific name	*Andrographis paniculata*
Family	Acanthaceae

MEDICINAL WHEEL

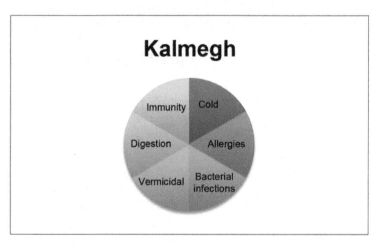

Also used in protecting liver and gall bladder, prevents acne.

GROWING TIPS

 Bright Sun   Moderate feed

 Moderate water   Loamy soils

Annona squamosa (Custard apple)

Annona squamosa is a small tree with fragnant flowers, roundish shaped fruits with knobby apperance.

DISTRIBUTION

It is native to west Indies and Tropical America. It is naturalized in India, Indonesia, Thailand, Taiwan and China.

Annona squamosa (Custard apple)

SUMMARY

Common Name	Custard apple
Height	Up to 18 feet
Flower	Green
Light	Bright Sun
Origin	West Indies, Tropical America
Scientific name	*Annona squamosa*
Family	Annonaceae

MEDICINAL WHEEL

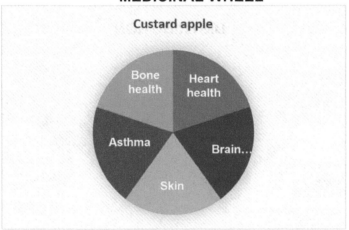

Also treats cancer, eye diseases, diabetes and digestive problems.

GROWING TIPS

 Bright Sun

 Moderate feed

 Moderate water

 Loamy soils

Antidesma ghaesembilla (Black currant tree)

Black currant tree is a tree which has grey bark, found in Tropical and subtropical Asia, north Australia, also Himalayas.

DISTRIBUTION

It is native to India, Sri Lanka, Bangladesh, China, Nepal, Cambodia, Indonesia, Loas, Malaysia, Mynamar, Phillipinnes, Thailand, Vietnam, Papau new Guinea and northern Australia.

Antidesma ghaesembilla (Black currant tree)

SUMMARY

Common Name	Black currant tree
Height	Up to 60 feet
Flower	Reddish yellow colour
Light	Bright Sun
Origin	India, Indo China, Australia
Scientific name	*Antidesma ghaesembilla* Gaertn.
Family	Phyllanthaceae

MEDICINAL WHEEL

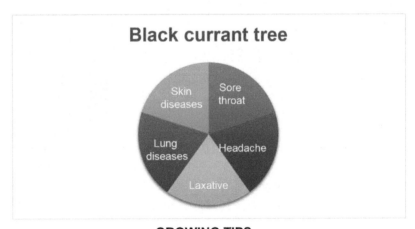

GROWING TIPS

 Bright Sun

 Moderate water

 Moderate feed

 Loamy soils

Argyreia nervosa (Elephant creeper)

Argyreia nervosa commonly referred to as "Elephant Creeper" is a perennial climbing vine.

DISTRIBUTION

■ Native
■ Naturalised

Argyreia nervosa is native to the Indian subcontinent and is naturalised in Africa and the Caribbean.

Argyreia nervosa (Elephant creeper)
SUMMARY

Common Name	Elephant Creeper / Vidhara
Height	Up to 30 feet
Flower	Blue, Pink, Purple colour
Light	Bright Sun
Origin	Indian subcontinent
Scientific name	*Argyreia nervosa*
Family	Convulvulaceae

MEDICINAL WHEEL

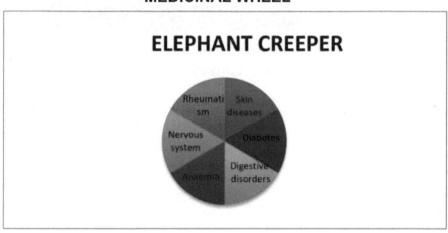

Roots are used as diuretic and an aphrodisiac, treats bacterial and viral infections and nervous system disorders.

GROWING TIPS

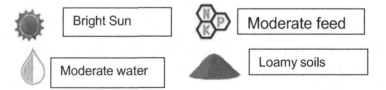

Ascelpias currasavica (Tropical milkweed)

Asclepias curassavica L. is commonly called as Tropical Milk Weed, Blood Flower Plant . It contains cardiac glycoside chemicals that are toxic, when eaten make the monarch butterflies and their larvae also toxic to predators, but they themselves are not harmed.

DISTRIBUTION

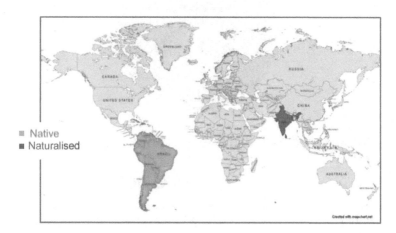

It is native to Central, South American and Caribbean. It is naturalised in India and Sri Lanka.

Ascelpias currasavica (Tropical milkweed)

SUMMARY

Common Name	Tropical Milk weed
Height	Up to 3 feet
Flower	Yellow/ Orange Red Colour
Light	Bright Sun
Origin	America
Scientific name	*Asclepias curassavica* L.
Family	Apocynaceae

MEDICINAL WHEEL

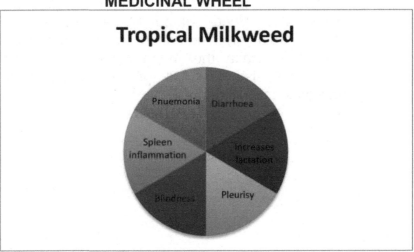

Also treats constipation, diabetes, blindness, pyoderma.

GROWING TIPS

 Bright Sun

 Low feed

 Low water

 Red /Sandy loam/ loamy

Asystasia gangetica (Chinese violet)

Asystasia gangetica called as Lavanavalli in sanskrit is a perennial species. It can be found along roadsides, cultivated areas and riverbanks as well as in semi- waterlogged areas.

DISTRIBUTION

■ Native
■ Naturalised

It is native to Malaysia, India and tropical Africa. It is naturalised Australia, including Queensland and Western Australia.

Asystasia gangetica (Chinese violet)

SUMMARY

Common Name	Chinese violet / Creeping foxglove
Height	Up to 1.8 feet
Flower	Purple and white colour
Light	Bright Sun, Semi shade
Origin	India, Malaysia
Scientific name	*Asystasia gangetica*
Family	Acanthaceae

MEDICINAL WHEEL

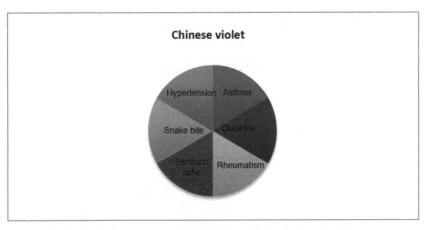

Chinese violet

It is used to cure childbirth pain, abdominal syndromes, colitis, microbial infections, haemorrhoids.

GROWING TIPS

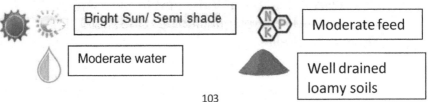

Bright Sun/ Semi shade

Moderate feed

Moderate water

Well drained loamy soils

Atrocarpus heterophyllus (Jackfruit)

Atrocarpus heterophyllus, commonly called jackfruit is known for producing the largest tree borne fruit which can weigh up to 40 kg.

DISTRIBUTION

It is native to India, Bangladesh and Malaysia

Atrocarpus heterophyllus (Jackfruit)

SUMMARY

Common Name	Jackfruit
Height	Up to 90 feet
Flower	Pale green colour
Light	Bright Sun
Origin	India, Bangladesh and Malaysia
Scientific name	*Atrocarpus heterophyllus* L.
Family	Moraceae

MEDICINAL WHEEL

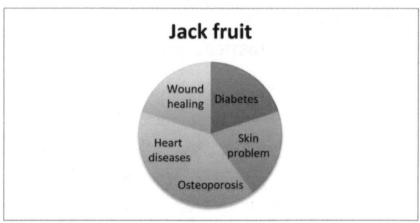

Also used to treat diabetes, wound healing, skin problems, heart diseases, osteoporosis and hair health.

GROWING TIPS

 Bright Sun

 Moderate feed

 Moderate water

 Loamy soils

Barleria prionitis (Porcupine flower)

Barleria prionitis commonly called as Porcupine flower or Vajradanti is an evergreen prickly shrub.

DISTRIBUTION

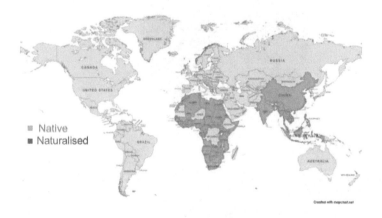

The native of Barleria is India, South East Asia, China and parts of Africa

Barleria prionitis (Porcupine flower)

SUMMARY

Common Name	Porcupine Flower / Vajradanthi
Height	Up to 5.5 ft
Flower	Yellow/ Golden Yellow Flower
Light	Bright sun
Origin	Indian subcontinent
Scientific name	*Barleria prionitis*
Family	Acanthaceae

MEDICINAL WHEEL

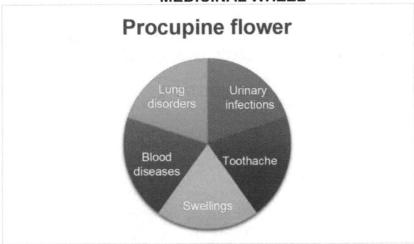

Also used as an analgesic, anaemia, diabetes and antidote for snake bites.

GROWING TIPS

 Bright Sun/ Semi shade   Moderate feed

 Moderate water   Well drained loamy soils

Barleria strigosa (Bristly Blue Barleria)

Barleria strigosa is commonly known as Bristly blue barleria is a plant in the family Acanthaceae.

DISTRIBUTION

■ Native
■ Naturalised

It is native to Indian subcontinent, Indochina and China. It is naturalised in Australia.

Barleria strigosa (Bristly Blue Barleria)
SUMMARY

Common Name	Bristly Blue barleria
Height	Up to 3 feet
Flower	Blue / Purplish
Light	Bright Sun
Origin	Indian subcontinent
Scientific name	*Barleria stirgosa*
Family	Acanthaceae

MEDICINAL WHEEL

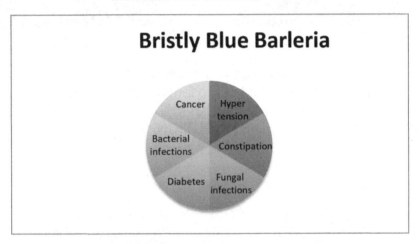

Also treats inflammation, ulcer, Hepatprotective, analgesic and antiviral.

GROWING TIPS

 Bright Sun

 Moderate feed

 Moderate water

 Red/ loamy soils

Bauhinia tomentosa (Yellow Bell Orchid Tree)

Bauhinia tomentosa commonly called as yellow bauhinia or yellow bell orchid tree is a species of plant in the family Fabaceae.

DISTRIBUTION

■ Native
■ Naturalised

Bauhinia tomentosa is native to India, Sri Lanka, Bangladesh, Zamia, Zimbabwe, South Africa, Tanzania, Kenya, Ethiopia and Somalia.

Bauhinia tomentosa (Yellow Bell Orchid Tree)

SUMMARY

Common Name	Yellow Bell Orchid Tree
Height	Up to 12 feet
Flower	Yellow Colour
Light	Bright Sun
Origin	Indian Subcontinent, Africa
Scientific name	*Bauhinia tomentosa*
Family	Fabaceae

MEDICINAL WHEEL

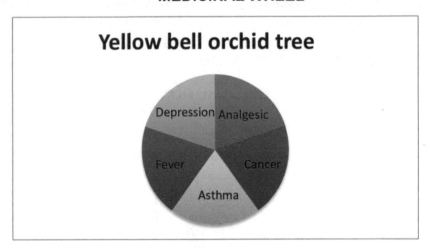

Also used to treat   bacterial infections, tumours, liver inflammations

GROWING TIPS

 Bright Sun   Moderate feed

 Moderate water   Red soils

Borassus flabellifer (Palmyra palm)

Borassus flabellifer is a roboust tree known for its large, fan shaped leaves.

DISTRIBUTION

It is native to Indian subcontinent and Southeast Asia, New Guinea and northern Australia. It is naturalized in Pakistan and parts of China.

Borassus flabellifer (Palmyra palm)

SUMMARY

Common name	Palmyra palm/ Toddy palm/ Fan palm
Height	Up to 90 feet tall
Flower colour	Cream/ Off white
Light	Bright Sun
Origin	Indian subcontinent, Southeast Asia, Australia
Scientific name	*Borassus flabellifer*
Family	Arecaceae

MEDICINAL WHEEL

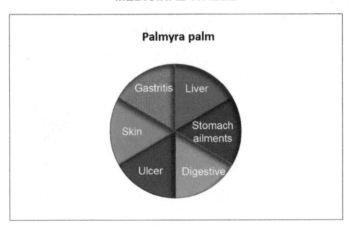

It is used to treat respiratory disorders, microbial infections and used as a sweetener for diabetic patients.

GROWING TIPS

 Bright Sun

 Moderate feed

 Moderate water

 Loamy soils

Breynia vitis idaea (Indian snow berry)

Breynia vitis-idaea is known as the Indian snow berry is a perennial tree-like species.

DISTRIBUTION

■ Native
■ Naturalised
—

It is native to Indian sub continent ,Southern China and Indonesia.

Breynia vitis idaea (Indian snow berry)

SUMMARY

Common Name	Indian Snow Berry/ Snow bush
Height	Up to 6 Feet
Flower	Yellow colour, Green
Light	Bright Sun
Origin	Indian subcontinent
Scientific name	*Breynia vitis-idaea*
Family	Phyllanthaceae

MEDICINAL WHEEL

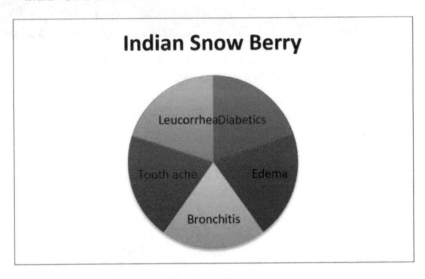

Also used as mouthwash, prevents hemorrhage, headaches and cancer.

GROWING TIPS

 Bright Sun

 Moderate feed

Low water

 Red / loamy soils

Buddleja asiatica L. (Asian butterfly Bush)

Buddleja asiatica is a tender deciduous shrub.

DISTRIBUTION

■ Native
■ Naturalised

It is native to East Indies, including India, Nepal, Bangladesh, China, Taiwan, Burma, Thailand, Laos, Cambodia, Vietnam and Malaysia.

Buddleja asiatica (Asian Butterflu Bush)

SUMMARY

Common Name	Asian butterfly Bush
Height	Up to 6 feet
Flower	White/Pale yellow / Cream
Light	Bright Sun/ Semi shade
Origin	Indian Subcontinent
Scientific name	*Buddleja asiatica* L.
Family	Scrophulariaceae

MEDICINAL WHEEL

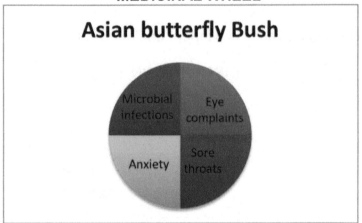

Also used as a pain reliever, treats inflammations, diarrhoea,, asthma and diabetes.

GROWING TIPS

 Bright Sun/ Semi shade   Moderate feed

 Moderate water   Sandy loam/ loamy

Caesalpinia pulcherrima (Peacock flower)

Caesalpinia pulcherrima is commonly known as Peacock flower is a flowering plant.

DISTRIBUTION

■ Native
■ Naturalised

It is native to West Indies , Mexico and America and is naturalised in the Indian sub continent .

Caesalpinia pulcherrima (Peacock flower)

SUMMARY

Common Name	Peacock Flower/ Red bird of Paradise
Height	Up to 18 feet
Flower	Red / Golden Red Colour
Light	Bright Sun
Origin	America and West Indies
Scientific name	*Caesalpinia pulcherrima*
Family	Fabaceae

MEDICINAL WHEEL

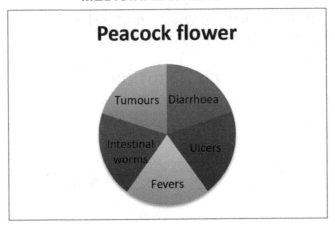

Also used to treat inflammation.

GROWING TIPS

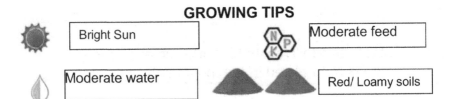

Bright Sun

Moderate feed

Moderate water

Red/ Loamy soils

Calotropis procera (Apple of Sodom)

Calotropis procera is commonly known as Sodom apple or Giant milkweed is a species of flowering plant.

DISTRIBUTION

■ Native
■ Naturalised

It is native to North Africa, South Asia, Middle East and Indochina.

Calotropis procera (Apple of Sodom)
SUMMARY

Common Name	Sodom apple / Giant Milkweed
Height	Up to 13 feet
Flower	Cream / Off-White, Purple, White
Light	Bright Sun
Origin	Indo-china and Middle East
Scientific name	*Calotropis procera*
Family	Apocynaceae

MEDICINAL WHEEL

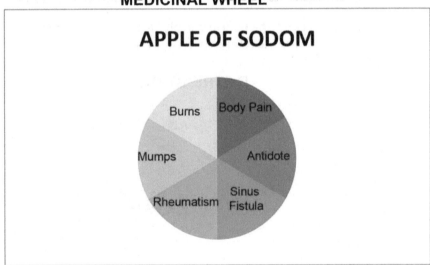

Also use as an antidote for snake bite, worm infestations, ulcers, jaundice.

GROWING TIPS

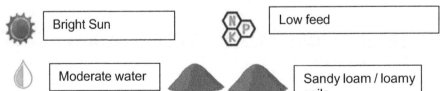

Caryota urens (Fishtail Palm)

Caryota urens is commonly known as Fishtail Palm is known for its unique bipinnate leaves that resembles a fish tail.

DISTRIBUTION

■ Native
■ Naturalised

It is native to India, Sri Lanka, Southern China and Northern Australia.

Caryota urens (Fishtail Palm)

SUMMARY

Common Name	Fishtail palm
Height	Up to 30 feet
Flower	Cream/ Off white
Light	Bright Sun/ Semi shade
Origin	India, Sri Lanka, China and Australia
Scientific name	*Caryota urens* L.
Family	Arecaceae

MEDICINAL WHEEL

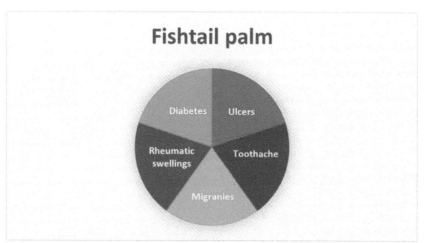

Also used to treat boils, urinary disorders and antidote for snake bites.

GROWING TIPS

  Bright Sun/ Semi shade   Moderate feed

 Moderate water   Loamy soils

Cassia auriculata (Avaram senna)

Cassia auriculata is commonly called avaram or tanner's cassia is a small to medium-sized shrub. It is well-known for producing a show-stopping bloom of yellow flowers in May-June/July.

DISRTIBUTION

■ Native
■ Naturalised

It is native to Sri Lanka, India and Burma.

Cassia auriculata (Avaram senna)

SUMMARY

Common Name	Avaram, Tanner's cassia or Matura Tea
Height	Up to 3 - 4 feet
Flower	Yellow / Golden
Light	Bright Sun
Origin	India, Sri Lanka
Scientific name	*Cassia auriculata*
Family	Fabaceae

MEDICINAL WHEEL

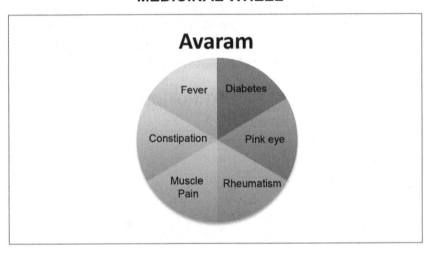

Also used to treat hyperglycemia, hyperlipidemia and bacterial infections.

GROWING TIPS

 Bright Sun

 Moderate feed

 Moderate water

 Loamy soils

Cassia fistula L. (Golden shower)

Cassia fistula L. is known as golden shower, purging cassia, Indian laburnum, kanikonna or pudding-pipe tree is a flowering plant.

DISTRIBUTION

■ Native
■ Naturalised

It is native to Indian subcontinent and South East Asia.

Cassia fistula L. (Golden shower)

SUMMARY

Common Name	Golden Shower / Indian Laburnum
Height	Up to 50 feet
Flower	Yellow / Golden colour
Light	Bright Sun
Origin	Indian subcontinent
Scientific name	*Cassia fistula* L.
Family	Fabaceae

MEDICINAL WHEEL

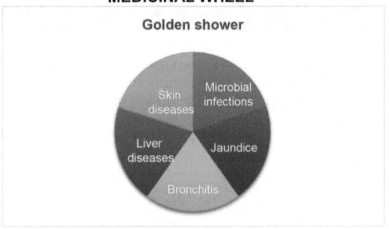

Golden shower

Also acts as an anti tumour and treats gout.

GROWING TIPS

 Bright Sun/ Semi shade   Low feed

Moderate water    Red /Sandy loam/ loamy

Centella asiatica (Indian pennywort)

Centella asiatica is a perennial plant in the family Apiaceae. The plant has small and fan shaped leaves.

DISTRIBUTION

■ . Native
■ Naturalised

It is native to subtropical and tropical regions of Asia and Africa. It is native to India, China, Indonesia, Malaysia, Sri Lanka, South Africa and Madagascar.

Centella asiatica (Indian pennywort)

SUMMARY

Common Name	Indian pennywort
Height	Up to 1.5 feet
Flower	White Colour
Light	Bright Sun/ Semi shade
Origin	Asia and Africa
Scientific name	*Centella asiatica* L.
Family	Apiaceae

MEDICINAL WHEEL

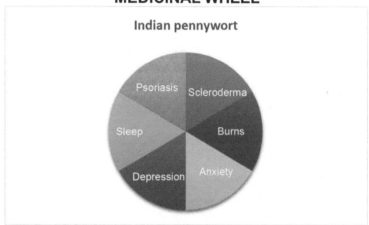

Also used to treat ulcers and protects central nervous system.

GROWING TIPS

 Bright Sun/ Semi shade   Moderate feed

 High water   Loamy soils

Cestrum diurnum (Day blooming jasmine)

Cestrum diurnum is commonly known as day blooming jasmine which has about 150-250 species of flowering plants.

DISTRIBUTION

It is native to the West Indies and naturalised in South Asia.

Cestrum diurnum (Day blooming jasmine)

SUMMARY

Common Name	Day-blooming jasmine.
Height	Up to 12 feet
Flower	White
Light	Bright Sun
Origin	West Indies
Scientific name	*Cestrum diurnum*
Family	Solanaceae

MEDICINAL WHEEL

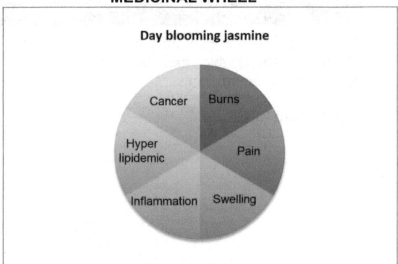

Day blooming jasmine

Also used to treat psoriasis, diabetes and microbial infections.

GROWING TIPS

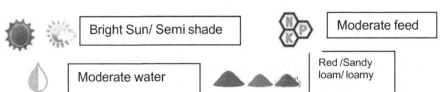

Bright Sun/ Semi shade

Moderate feed

Moderate water

Red /Sandy loam/ loamy

Chamaecostus cuspidatus (Insulin plant)

Chamaecostus cuspidatus is commonly called as fiery costus or Insulin plant. In India, it is known as insulin plant for its anti-diabetic properties.It is a perennial plant.

DISTRIBUTION

■ Native
■ Naturalised

It is native to Eastern Brazil and is naturalised in India.

Chamaecostus cuspidatus (Insulin plant)

SUMMARY

Common Name	Costus / Insulin Plant/ Spiral
Height	2 Feet
Flower	Yellow or Orange
Light	Bright sun, Semi shade
Origin	Eastern Brazil
Scientific name	*Chamaecostus cuspidatus*
Family	Costaceae

MEDICINAL WHEEL

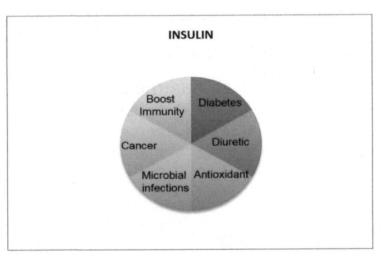

Also used to treat renal disorders, inflammations.

GROWING TIPS

 Bright Sun/ Semi shade

 Low feed

 Moderate water

 Well drained loamy soils

Cheilocostus speciosus (Crepe Ginger)

Costus is commonly referred to as Kushta /Crepe ginger is a tall landscape plant with large dark green leaves arranged on the stalk in spiral.

DISTRIBUTION

- Native
- Naturalised

It is native to tropical and subtropical regions of Asia, Africa and America.

Cheilocostus speciosus (Crepe Ginger)

SUMMARY

Common Name	Kushta (Crepe ginger)
Height	Up to 6.5 feet
Flower	Red, Yellow Orange and White colour
Light	Semi shade, Shade
Origin	Indian subcontinent and Southeast Asia.
Scientific name	*Cheilocostus speciosus*
Family	Costaceae

MEDICINAL WHEEL

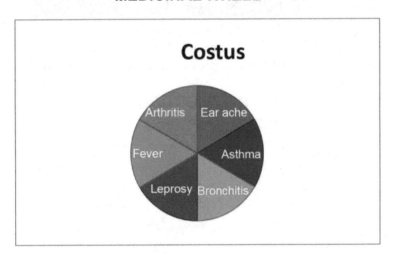

Also used to treat diabetes, parasitic worms, diarrhoea,giddiness,gastritis,rheumatoid arthritis.

GROWING TIPS

  Semi shade/ Complete shade   Low feed

 Moderate water    Red /Sandy loam/ loamy

Chrysopogon zizanioides (Vetiver)

Chrysopogon zizanioides is commonly known as vetiver and khus is a perennial bunchgrass.

DISTRIBUTION

■ Native
■ Naturalised

It is native to India, Bangladesh and Burma.

Chrysopogon zizanioides (Vetiver)

SUMMARY

Common Name	Vetiver /Khus
Height	Up to 6 feet
Flower	Purple, Silver/ Grey
Light	Bright Sun
Origin	India
Scientific name	*Chrysopogon zizanioides*
Family	Poaceae

MEDICINAL WHEEL

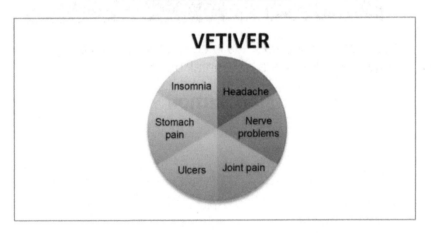

Also used to prevent acne and pimples, relieve inflammations, anxiety and stress, improves skin, hair and sleep.

GROWING TIPS

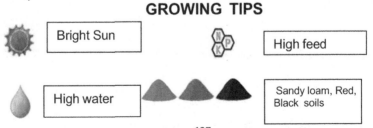

Bright Sun

High feed

High water

Sandy loam, Red, Black soils

Cinnamomum verum (Dalchini)

Cinnamomum verum is commonly known as Dalchini is an evergreen tree characterized by oval-shaped leaves, thick bark and berry fruit.

DISTRIBUTION

■ Native
■ Naturalised

It is native to India and Sri Lanka.

Cinnamomum verum (Dalchini)

SUMMARY

Common Name	Dalchini
Height	Up to 30-50 feet
Flower	White, Cream or off white
Light	Bright sun
Origin	India
Scientific name	*Cinnamomum verum*
Family	Lauraceae

MEDICINAL WHEEL

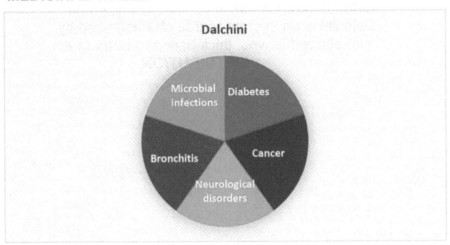

Also as an anti-inflammatory, and cardiovascular disease lowering compound.

GROWING TIPS

Bright Sun	High feed
Moderate water	Loamy soils

Cissus quadrangularis (Veldt Grape)

Cissus quadrangularis commonly known as Veldt grape, Devils backbone or adamant creeper is a climbing succulent known for its quadrangular, jointed stems.

DISTRIBUTION

■ Native
■ Naturalised

It is native to tropical Asia and Africa.

Cissus quadrangularis (Veldt Grape)

SUMMARY

Common Name	Veldt Grape
Height	Up to15 feet
Flower	Pink or White
Light	Semi shade
Origin	Asia and Africa
Scientific name	*Cissus quadrangularis*
Family	Vitaceae

MEDICINAL WHEEL

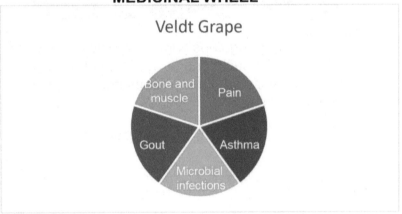

Also helps to treat inflammations, cancer, allergies, and cholestrol.

GROWING TIPS

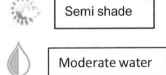 Semi shade

 Moderate feed

Moderate water

 Sandy soils

Citrus limon (Lemon)

The lemon is a species of small evergreen tree in the flowering plant family Rutaceae.

DISTRIBUTION

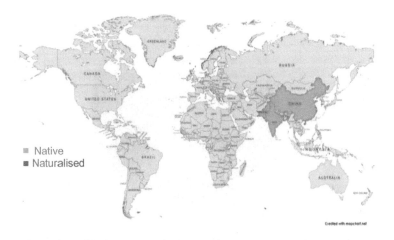

■ Native
■ Naturalised

It is native to Northeast India (Assam), parts of Pakistan and Southern China.

Citrus limon (Lemon)

SUMMARY

Common Name	Lemon
Height	15 to 20 Feet
Flower	White
Light	Bright Sun, Semishade
Origin	India
Scientific name	*Citrus limon*
Family	Rutaceae

MEDICINAL WHEEL

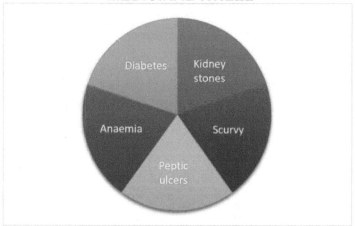

Also helps to treat respiratory disorders, eye infections, heart diseases and even very high fever.

GROWING TIPS

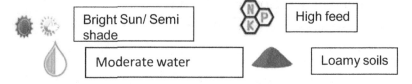

Clerodendrum indicum (Tube Flower)

Clerodendrum indicum is commonly known as Tube flower or Turks Turban is a landscape weed.

DISTRIBUTION

■ Native
■ Naturalised

It is native to temperate and tropical Asia from China to the Philippines.

Clerodendrum indicum (Tube Flower)

SUMMARY

Common Name	Tube Flower/ Turks Turban
Height	Up to 6 feet
Flower	White
Light	Bright sun, Partial shade
Origin	Asia
Scientific name	*Clerodendrum indicum*
Family	Lamiaceae

MEDICINAL WHEEL

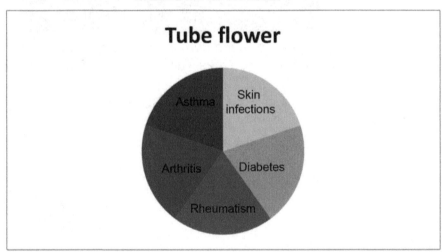

Also used to treat inflammations, dropsy, swellings, edema, gout.

GROWING TIPS

 Bright Sun/ Semi shade

 Moderate feed

 High water

 Loamy soils

Clitoria ternatea (Butterfly pea)

Clitoria ternatea commonly called as Butterfly pea is a perennial vine.

DISTRIBUTION

It is native to South East Asia and is naturalised in India.

Clitoria ternatea (Butterfly pea)

SUMMARY

Common Name	Blue Pea/ Butterfly pea
Height	Up to 15 feet
Flower	Blue and White
Light	Bright, Direct Sunlight
Origin	South East Asia
Scientific name	*Clitoria ternatea*
Family	Fabaceae

MEDICINAL WHEEL

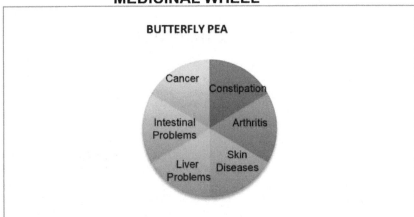

Also used to treat indigestion and hair care.

GROWING TIPS

 Bright Sun   Low feed

 Moderate water   Red soils

Colocasia esculenta (Taro)

Colocasia esculenta is known for its large heart shaped leaves and edible corms. Taro is staple food in many tropical regions..

DISTRIBUTION

- Native
- Naturalised

It is native to Indian subcontinent and Southeast Asia.

Colocasia esculenta (Taro)

SUMMARY

Common Name	Taro
Height	Up to 6 feet
Flower	Yellow green colour
Light	Semi shade
Origin	Indian subcontinent, Southeast Asia
Scientific name	*Colocasia esculenta*
Family	Araceae

MEDICINAL WHEEL

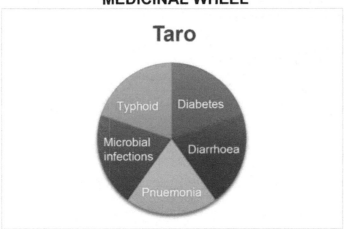

Also used to treat neuroblastoma, myocardial and Central Nervous System depression.

GROWING TIPS

 Semi shade   Moderate feed

 Moderate water   Sandy loam soils

Coleus amboinicus (Indian borage)

Coleus amboinicus is commonly called as Mexican mint, pudhina or Indian borage. It has a pungent oregano-like flavour and odour.

DISTRIBUTION

■ Native
■ Naturalised

Indian borage is native to east Africa, India and is naturalised in various parts of Great Britain, North America and Australia.

Coleus amboinicus (Indian borage)

SUMMARY

Common Name	Pudhina / Indian borage
Height	Up to 2 feet
FLower	Purple colour
Light	Bright Sun, Semi shade
Origin	India, Southern and Eastern Africa
Scientific Name	*Coleus amboinicus*
Family	Lamiaceae

MEDICINAL WHEEL

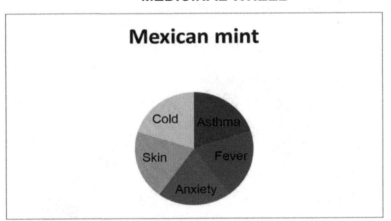

Mexican mint

Cold · Asthma · Fever · Anxiety · Skin

It can treat inflammation, swelling.

GROWING TIPS

Bright Sun/ Semi shade

Moderate water

Moderate feed

Sandy loam soils

Coleus zeylanicus (Iruveriya)

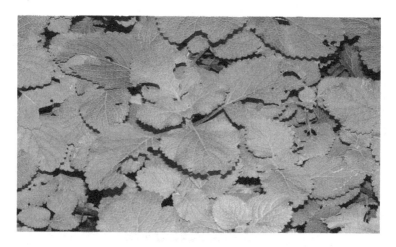

Coleus zeylanicus is an important aromatic medicinal plant that belongs to the family Lamiaceae.

DISTRIBUTION

■ Native
■ Naturalised

It is native range to tropical and subtropical Asia and to Northern Australia.

Coleus zeylanicus (Iruveriya)

SUMMARY

Common Name	Iruveriya
Height	Up to 1 Feet
Flower	Bluish to pale lavender
Light	Bright Sun, Semi shade
Origin	Malaysia /Thailand
Scientific name	*Coleus zeylanicus*
Family	Lamiaceae.

MEDICINAL USES

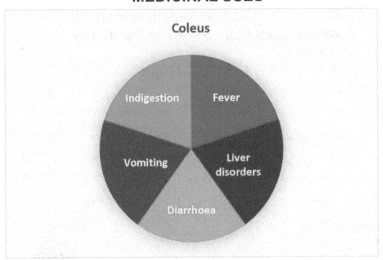

Also used to treat leuchoderma and urinal disorders.

GROWING TIPS

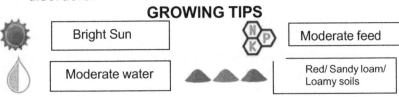

Bright Sun		Moderate feed
Moderate water		Red/ Sandy loam/ Loamy soils

Combretum indicum (Rangoon creeper)

Combretum indicum, commonly known as the Rangoon creeper or Burma creeper, is a vine with red flower clusters.

DISTRIBUTION

■ Native
■ Naturalised

It is native to Indian subcontinent, Myanmar, Malayasia and Phillipines.

Combretum indicum (Rangoon creeper)
SUMMARY

Common Name	Rangoon / Burma Creeper
Height	Up to 10 feet
Flower	Red and white colour
Light	Bright Sun
Origin	Indian subcontinent
Scientific name	*Combretum indicum*
Family	Combretaceae

MEDICINAL WHEEL

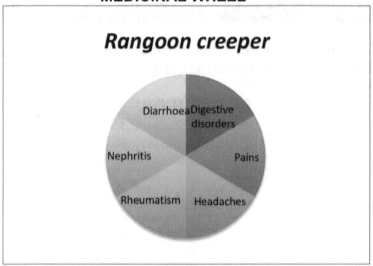

Also used to treat boils, ulcers, parasitic skin infections and fever.

GROWING TIPS

 Bright Sun
 Low feed
 Moderate water
 Loamy soils

Crinum sp. (Spider lily)

Crinum sp. is commonly known as Seashore Lily, Poison Bulb, Crinum Lily, Asiatic Poison Lily and Spider Lily. The entire plant is poisonous.

DISTRIBUTION

It is native to tropical and subtropical regions of Asia, Australia and America.

Crinum sp. (Spider lily)

SUMMARY

Common Name	Asiatic Poison Lily / Spider Lily
Height	2 to 4 feet
Flower	White, Pink and Red
Light	Bright Sun, semi shade
Origin	Indian subcontinent, South east Asia
Scientific name	*Crinum sp.*
Family	Amaryllidaceae

MEDICINAL WHEEL

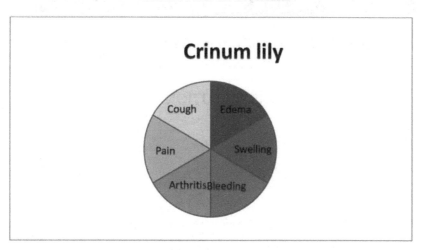

Also used to treat osteoarthritis. It can cure skin ulcers, redness, boils and injuries.

GROWING TIPS

 Bright Sun/ Semi shade   Moderate feed

 Moderate water   Sandy loam soils

Crossandra infundibuliformis (Crossandra)

Crossandra infundibuliformis commonly called the firecracker flower or firecracker plant.

DISTRIBUTION

■ Native
■ Naturalised

It is native to India, Sri Lanka, Kenya, Ethiopia, Republic of Congo

Crossandra infundibuliformis (Crossandra)

SUMMARY

Common Name	Firecracker Flower / Kanakabaram
Height	Up to 4 Feet
Flower	Orange / Yellow /Pink / Red colour
Light	Bright Sun
Origin	India, Sri Lanka
Scientific name	*Crossandra infundibuliformis*
Family	Acanthaceae

MEDICINAL WHEEL

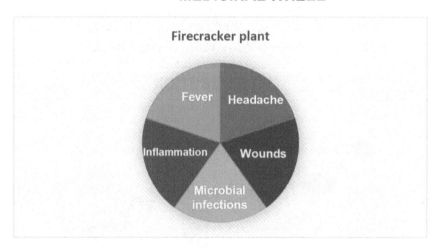

Firecracker plant

Fever / Headache / Wounds / Microbial infections / Inflammation

Also acts as aphrodisiac and analgesic and is rich in antioxidants.

GROWING TIPS

 Bright Sun

 Moderate feed

 Moderate water

 Red/ Loamy soils

Crotalaria retusa (Rattle weed)

Crotalaria retusa is a species of flowering plant in the legume family known by various common names including devil-bean, rattle weed, shack shack, and wedge- leaf rattle pod. It is poisonous to livestock and contaminates human food.

DISTRIBUTION

Crotalaria retusa is native to the Arabian Peninsula, Madagascar, India, Southeast Asia to Western Australia. It is naturalised throughout tropical Africa and tropical America.

Crotalaria retusa (Rattle weed)

SUMMARY

Common Name	Rattle weed
Height	Up to 5 Feet
Flower	Yellow
Light	Bright sun, Semi shade
Origin	India, SE Asia, Australia
Scientific name	*Crotalaria retusa*
Family	Fabaceae

MEDICINAL WHEEL

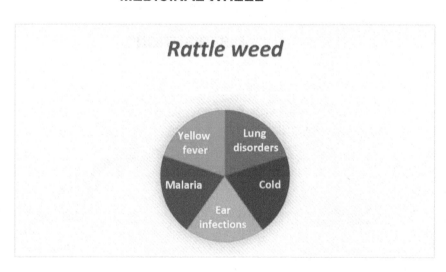

Also used to treat epidermal infections, haemoptysis, anti-inflammatory, antimicrobial, antioxidant, and antiproliferative.

GROWING TIPS

 Bright Sun/ Semi shade

 Low feed

 Moderate water

 Loamy soils

Curcuma longa (Turmeric)

Curcuma longa is commonly called Turmeric is extracted from the rhizome is an underground horizontal stem which resembles a tuberous root.

DISTRIBUTION

■ Native
■ Naturalised

It is native to tropical southeast Asia and south Asia.

Curcuma longa (Turmeric)
SUMMARY

Common Name	Turmeric
Height	Up to 3 feet
Flower	White, Yellow / Golden
Light	Bright Sun, Semi shade
Origin	Tropical South Asia, Southeast Asia
Scientific name	*Curcuma longa*
Family	Zingiberaceae

MEDICINAL WHEEL

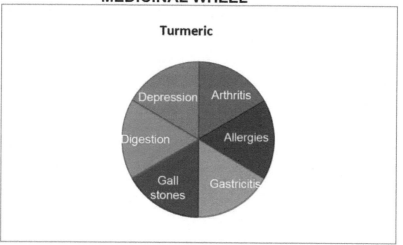

Also treats inflammation, skin disorders, respiratory tract problems, muscle soreness, cancer, flu, herpes and increases immunity.

GROWING TIPS

 Bright Sun/ Semi shade   Moderate feed

 High water   Loamy soils

Curcuma zedoaria (White turmeric)

Curcuma zedoaria is commonly called as white turmeric is a perennial rhizomatous herb.

DISTRIBUTION

- Native
- Naturalised

It is native to Southeast Asia and is now naturalised in United States.

Curcuma zedoaria (White turmeric)

SUMMARY

Common Name	White turmeric
Height	Up to 3 Feet
Flower	White/ Yellow to shades of pink
Light	Bright sun, Semi shade
Origin	Asia
Scientific name	*Curcuma zedoaria*
Family	Zingiberaceae

MEDICINAL WHEEL

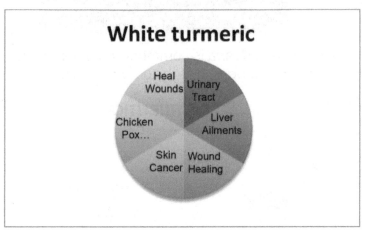

Also used as rheumatoid arthritis, chronic anterior uveitis, conjunctivitis.

GROWING TIPS

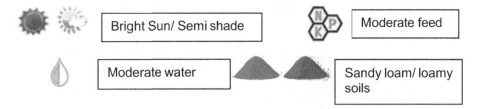

Decalepis hamiltonii (Swallow root)

Decalepis hamiltonii is a species of plant in the family Apocynaceae.

DISTRIBUTION

It is native to Peninsular India .

Decalepis hamiltonii (Swallow root)

SUMMARY

Common Name	Swallow root / Makali beru
Height	Up to 2 feet
Flower	Yellow
Light	Bright Sun
Origin	Southern Peninsular India
Scientific name	*Decalepis hamiltonii*
Family	Apocynaceae

MEDICINAL WHEEL

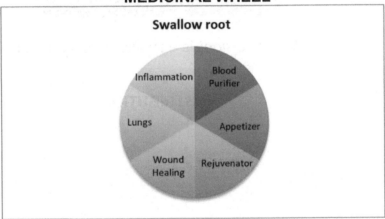

Also used in treatment of diseases related to the digestive system, skin diseases, circulatory system, fever .

GROWING TIPS

 Bright Sun

 Moderate feed

 Moderate water

 Well drained loamy soils

Gloriosa superba L. (Glory lily)

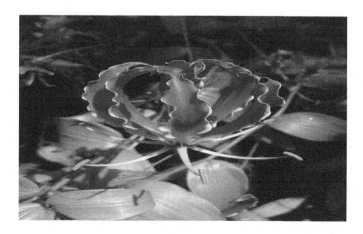

Gloriosa superba is a species of flowering plant commonly called as flame lily, climbing lily, creeping lily, glory lily, gloriosa lily, tiger claw and fire lily.

DISTRIBUTION

■ Native
■ Naturalised

It is native to sub-Saharan, South Africa, India, China, Bangladesh, Myanmar, Nepal and Madagascar. It is naturalised in Australia.

Gloriosa superba L. (Glory lily)

SUMMARY

Common Name	Glory Lily
Height	Up to 10 feet
Flower	Bright Red to orange Colour, Yellow/ Golden
Light	Bright sun, Semi shade
Origin	Indian Subcontinent / Africa/ China
Scientific name	*Gloriosa superba*
Family	Colchicaceae

MEDICINAL WHEEL

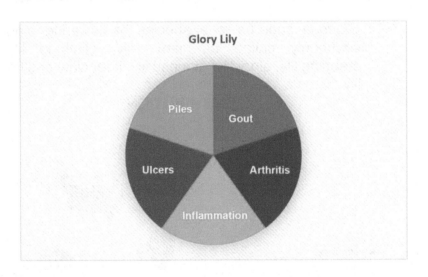

Glory Lily

Also used to cure indigestion, fever, infections, spasms, rheumatism, and antidote to snake bites.

GROWING TIPS

 Bright Sun/ Semi shade   Moderate feed

 Moderate water   Loamy soils

Gymnema sylvestre (Gurmar)

Gymnema sylvestre is a perennial woody vine. Common names include gymnema, Australian cow plant, and the Hindi term gurmar, which means "sugar destroyer".

DISTRIBUTION

■ Native
■ Naturalised

It is native to India, Africa and Australia.

Gymnema sylvestre (Gurmar)

SUMMARY

Common Name	Gurmar
Height	Up to 9 Feet
Flower	Pale pink, Yellow
Light	Bright Sun
Origin	Southern Peninsular India,
Scientific name	*Gymnema sylvestre*
Family	Apocynaceae

MEDICINAL WHEEL

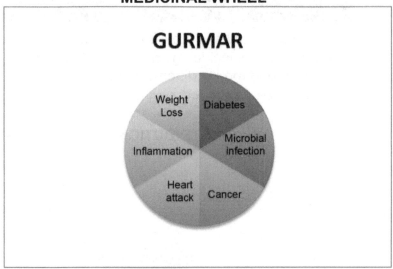

Also helps in treating cancer, helps in weight loss, reduces risk of heart attack and inflammation

GROWING TIPS

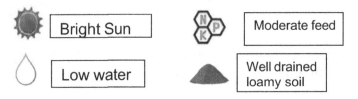

Bright Sun

Low water

Moderate feed

Well drained loamy soil

Hedychium coronarium (Butterfly ginger)

Hedychium coronarium commonly called white ginger lily or garland flower is a rhizomatous tender perennial.

DISTRIBUTION

■ Native
■ Naturalised

It is native to the Himalayas of India (Sikkim and Tripura), Bangladesh, Nepal, Bhutan, Myanmar, Thailand, southern China, Taiwan and Vietnam.

Hedychium coronarium (Butterfly ginger)

SUMMARY

Common Name	Butterfly Ginger
Height	3-6 feet tall
Flower	White, Yellow / Golden
Light	Bright sun, Semi shade
Origin	Indian, Asia, China
Scientific name	*Hedychium coronarium*
Family	Zingiberaceae

MEDICINAL WHEEL

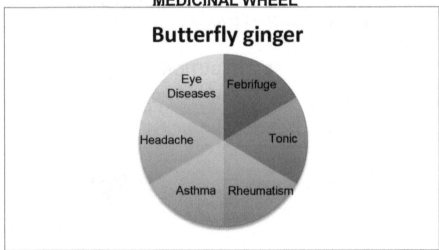

Also used as a arthritis, bronchitis, gastric diseases, cuts, swelling and fever.

GROWING TIPS

 Bright Sun/ Semi shade   Low feed

 High water   Loamy soils

Helicteres isora (Indian screw tree)

Helicteres isora sometimes called the Indian screw tree is a small tree assigned to the family Malvaceae.

DISTRIBUTION

■ Native
■ Naturalised

It is native to Asia including India, Pakistan, Nepal, Myanmar, Thailand, Sri Lanka, South China, Malay Peninsula, Saudi Arabia and Australia.

Helicteres isora (Indian screw tree)

SUMMARY

Common Name	Indian screw tree
Height	Up to 15 feet
Flower	Light Green, Red colour
Light	Bright Sun
Origin	Indian subcontinent, China and Australia
Scientific name	*Helicteres isora*
Family	Malvaceae

MEDICINAL USES

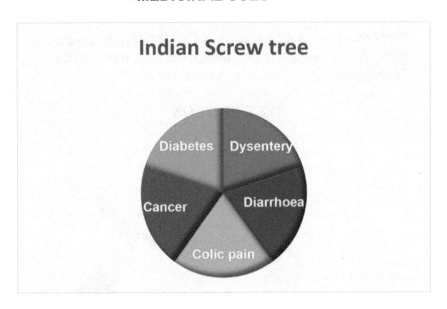

Also used to treat gastrointestinal disorders.

GROWING TIPS

 Bright Sun

 Moderate feed

 Moderate water

 Loamy soils

Hibiscus sp. (Hibiscus)

Hibiscus is a genus of flowering plants, quite large comprising several hundred species that are native to subtropical and tropical regions throughout the world.

DISTRIBUTION

It is native to Mauritius, Madagascar, Fiji, India, China. It is naturalised in Sri Lanka, Thailand, South Africa, Philippines, Myanmar and Pakistan.

Hibiscus sp. (Hibiscus)

SUMMARY

Common Name	Hibiscus
Height	Up to 16 feet
Flower	Red, Pink, White, Orange , Yellow ,Blue
Light	Bright Sun
Origin	Indian subcontinent
Scientific name	Hibiscus sp.
Family	Malvaceae.

MEDICINAL WHEEL

Hibiscus

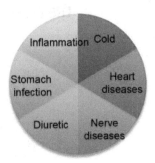

Also used to treat disorders of circulation, for dissolving phlegm.

GROWING TIPS

 Bright Sun

 Moderate water

 Moderate feed

Well drained loamy soil

Holarrhena pubescens (Ivory tree)

Holarrhena pubescens is a species of flowering plant in the family Apocynaceae.

DISTRIBUTION

■ Native
■ Naturalised

It is native to central and southern Africa, the Indian Subcontinent, Indochina and parts of China.

Holarrhena pubescens (Ivory tree)

SUMMARY

Common Name	Ivory Tree, Easter tree, Bitter Oleander
Height	Up to 40 Feet
Flower	White
Light	Bright sun, Semi shade
Origin	Southern Africa, India subcontinent, China
Scientific name	*Holarrhena pubescens*
Family	Apocynaceae

MEDICINAL USES

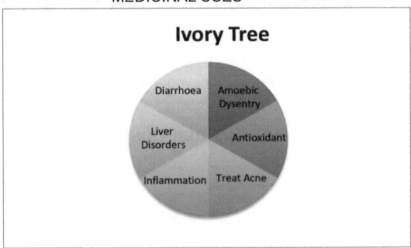

Also used in treating bronchitis, skin diseases, urinary troubles, irritable bowel syndrome and bleeding piles.

GROWING TIPS

 Bright sun, Semi shade

 Moderate feed

 Moderate water

 Sandy loamy soils

Hypericum mysorense (Goat weed)

Hypericum mysorense is a species of flowering plant in the Hypericaceae family commonly called as St. John's wort (SJW) or Goat weed it is a sprawling leafy herb.

DISTRIBUTION

■ Native
■ Naturalised

It is native to India and Sri Lanka .

Hypericum mysorense (Goat weed)

SUMMARY

Common Name	SJW / Goat Weed
Height	Up to 2 meters
Flower	Yellow colour
Light	Bright Sun, Semi shade
Origin	India and Sri Lanka
Scientific name	*Hypericum mysorense*
Family	Hypericaceae

MEDICINAL WHEEL

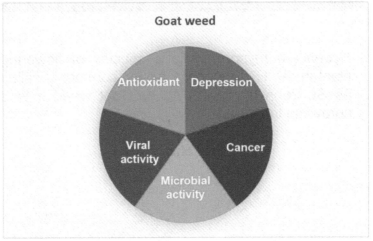

Also used in treating AIDS.

GROWING TIPS

 Bright Sun/ Semi shade   Moderate feed

 Moderate water   Loamy soils

Impatiens balsamina (Balsam)

Impatiens balsamina is a annual herb with serrated margins and showy flowers.

DISTRIBUTION

■ Native
■ Naturalised

It is native to India, Sri Lanka and tropical Asia.

Impatiens balsamina (Balsam)
SUMMARY

Common name	Garden balsam/ Rose balsam
Height	Up to 3 feet tall
Flower colour	Pink, Purple, Red, White and Orange
Light	Bright Sun/ Semi shade
Origin	India, Sri Lanka, Tropical Asia
Scientific name	*Impatiens balsamina*
Family	Balsaminaceae

MEDICINAL WHEEL

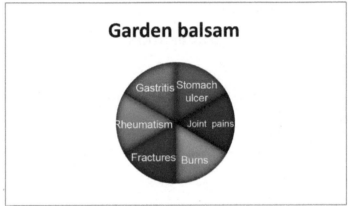

Also treats constipation, stomach cancer, scalds, warts and snakebites.

GROWING TIPS

Indigofera tinctoria (True indigo)

Indigofera tinctoria is a perennial shrub which is historically significant for its use in producing indigo dye.

DISTRIBUTION

■ Native
■ Naturalised

It is native to Indian subcontinent, Southeast Asia, West Africa, Tanzania to South Africa.

Indigofera tinctoria (True indigo)

SUMMARY

Common name	True indigo
Height	Up to 6 feet tall
Flower colour	Purple
Light	Bright Sun
Origin	South east Asia and Africa
Scientific name	*Indigofera tinctoria*
Family	Fabaceae

MEDICINAL WHEEL

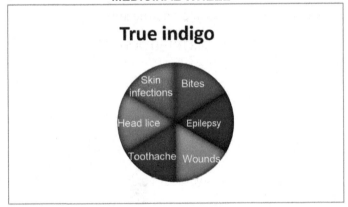

Also treats syphilis and gonorrhoea.

GROWING TIPS

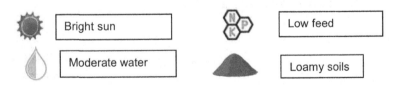

Ixora sp. (Jungle geranium)

Ixora is Latinized from *Ishwara* (Shiva- Hindu God). Ixora is commonly referred to as jungle geranium as it is a hardy plant.

DISTRIBUTION

■ Native
■ Naturalised

It is native to the India, Sri Lanka and Bangladesh.

Ixora sp. (Jungle geranium)

SUMMARY

Common Name	Jungle geranium, Jungle flame, Needle flower
Height	2 Feet
Flower	White, Cream yellow, Pink, Orange and Red
Light	Bright Sun
Origin	India
Scientific name	Ixora sp.
Family	Rubiaceae.

MEDICINAL WHEEL

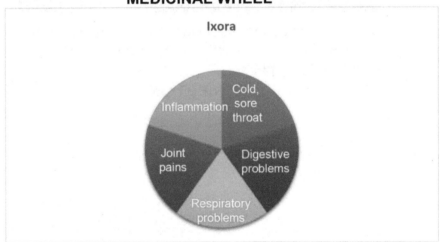

Also used to treat dysentery and catarrhal bronchitis, eczema and chronic ulcers.

GROWING TIPS

 Bright Sun   Moderate feed

 Moderate water   Well drained loamy soils

Justicia gendarussa (Willow leaved justicia)

Justicia gendarussa is commonly known as Willow-leaved justicia, Warer willow or Gardarusa. It is a perennial plant.

DISTRIBUTION

■ Native
■ Naturalised

It is native to Tropical Asia and China.

Justicia gendarussa (Willow leaved justicia)
SUMMARY

Common Name	Willow leaved Justicia / Warer willow/ Gardarusa
Height	3 Feet
Flower	White or pink with purple spots
Light	Bright sun, Semi shade
Origin	Tropical Asia, China
Scientific name	*Justicia gendarussa*
Family	Acanthaceae

MEDICINAL WHEEL

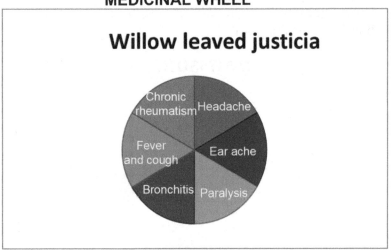

Also used to treat bruises.

GROWING TIPS

 Bright Sun/ Semi shade

 Moderate feed

 Moderate water

 Well drained Loamy soils

Kalanchoe pinnata L. (Cathedral bells)

Kalanchoe pinnata is commonly known as cathedral bells, air plant and love bush is a succulent plant.

DISTRIBUTION

- Native
- Naturalised

It is native to Madagascar, Fiji and naturalised in India.

Kalanchoe pinnata L. (Cathedral bells)

SUMMARY

Common Name	Cathedral bells
Height	Up to 6 Feet
Flower	Red, Pink, Cream, White
Light	Bright sun, Semi shade
Origin	Madagascar
Scientific name	*Kalanchoe pinnata* L.
Family	Crassulaceae

MEDICINAL WHEEL

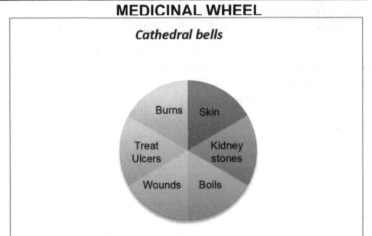

Cathedral bells

Also used to heal sores, treat smallpox. Leaf paste applied to chest to relieve coughs and headaches.

GROWING TIPS

  Bright Sun/ Semi shade Moderate feed

 Moderate water Sandy loam/ loamy soils

Kleinia grandiflora (Leafy cactus)

Kleinia grandiflora is an ayurvedic medicinal plant listed under endangered species.

DISTRIBUTION

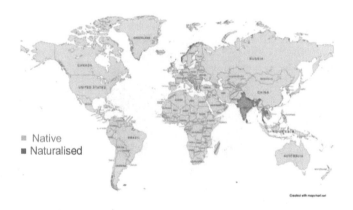

It is native to Indian subcontinent, southwest India, Sri Lanka, Nepal and northern Thailand.

Kleinia grandiflora (Leafy cactus)

SUMMARY

Common	Large flower Kleinia / Leafy cactus
Height	Up to 3 feet
Flower	Cream / Off-White, Green - Light Green
Light	Bright Sun, Semi shade
Origin	Indian subcontinent
Scientific name	*Kleinia grandiflora*
Family	Asteraceae

MEDICINAL WHEEL

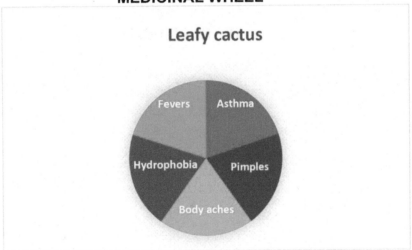

Leafy cactus

- Fevers
- Asthma
- Hydrophobia
- Pimples
- Body aches

Also used to treat swelling, bone fractures, dental issues.

GROWING TIPS

  Bright Sun/ Semi shade   Moderate feed

 Moderate water   Fertile loamy soils

Leea indica (Bandicoot berry)

Leea indica is a large shrub in the family Vitaceae.

DISTRIBUTION

- Native
- Naturalised

It is natively distributed in South Asia including India, Sri Lanka, Nepal, Bangladesh, Andaman and Nicobar Islands, Thailand, Indochina, southern China, through Peninsular Malaysia, Singapore, Philippines, Indonesia, New Guinea and northern Australia and Fiji.

Leea indica (Bandicoot berry)

SUMMARY

Common Name	Bandicoot Berry/ Common tree vine
Height	Up to 45 feet
Flower	Green / Yellow/ Golden
Light	Bright Sun, Semi shade
Origin	Indian subcontinent / China / Malaysia
Scientific name	*Leea indica*
Family	Vitaceae

MEDICINAL WHEEL

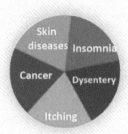

Bandicoot berry

Skin diseases — Insomnia — Dysentery — Itching — Cancer

Also used for treating body pains, eczema, malaria, intestinal and uterus cancer and vertigo.

GROWING TIPS

Bright Sun/ Semi shade

Moderate water

Moderatefeed

Fertile loamy

Leucas aspera (Thumbai)

Leucas aspera is commonly known as Thumbai is an annual herbaceous plant.

DISTRIBUTION

It is native to tropical and subtropical Asia, Mauritius.

Leucas aspera (Thumbai)

SUMMARY

Common Name	Thumbai
Height	Up to 2 feet
Flower	White
Light	Bright Sun
Origin	Tropical and Subtropical Asia
Scientific name	*Leucas aspera*
Family	Lamiaceae

MEDICINAL USES

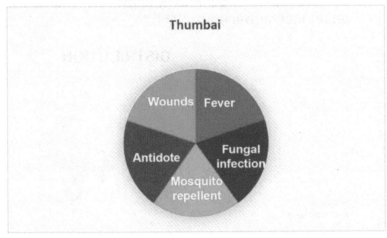

Thumbai

Wounds | Fever | Fungal infection | Mosquito repellent | Antidote

GROWING TIPS

 Bright Sun

 Low feed

 Moderate water

 Well drained loamy soils

Mangifera indica (Mango)

Mangifera indica commonly known as mango is mainly grown in tropical and subtropical regions, the fruit is enjoyed worldwide.

DISTRIBUTION

It is native to Indo Burma region, eastern India, Southern China and Southeast Asia.

Mangifera indica (Mango)
SUMMARY

Common Name	Mango/ Mangga
Height	Up to 90 feet
Flower	White/ Yellow or golden
Light	Bright Sun
Origin	Indo Burma, India, China, Southeast Asia
Scientific name	*Mangifera indica* L.
Family	Anacardiaceae

MEDICINAL WHEEL

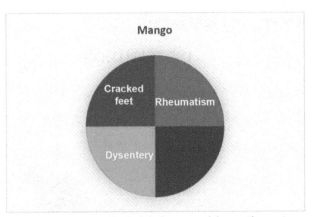

Also used to treat diphtheria, scabies, throat diseases, eruptions asthma.

GROWING TIPS

 Bright Sun

 Moderate feed

 Moderate water

 Loamy soils

Memecylon umbellatum (Cherry shrub)

Memecylon umbellatum commonly known as Ironwoon/ Anjani is a shrub in the family Melastomataceae.

DISTRIBUTION

■ Native
■ Naturalised

It is native to India, Sri Lanka, Myanmar, Thailand and Western Malaysia.

Memecylon umbellatum (Cherry shrub)
SUMMARY

Common Name	Ironwood / Anjani/ Cherry shrub
Height	Up to 9 feet
Flower	Blue
Light	Bright Sun, Semi shade
Origin	Indian subcontinent
Scientific name	*Memecylon umbellatum*
Family	Melastomataceae

MEDICINAL WHEEL

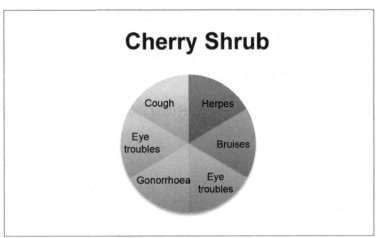

Also used to treat bruises, conjunctivitis, dyeing agent.

GROWING TIPS

 Bright Sun/ Semi shade

 Moderate feed

 Moderate water

 Loamy soils

Morus indica (Indian mulberry)

Morus indica commonly called as Indian Mulberry is a member of the genus Morus known for its edible fruits and often cultivated for its leaves.

DISTRIBUTION

It is native to Indian subcontinent and South East Asia.

Morus indica (Indian mulberry)

SUMMARY

Common Name	Indian Mulberry
Height	Up to 21 feet
Flower	Green colour
Light	Bright Sun
Origin	Indian subcontinent, Southeast Asia
Scientific name	*Morus indica*
Family	Moraceae

MEDICINAL WHEEL

Also used to treat fatigue, constipation, blood disorders and anemia.

GROWING TIPS

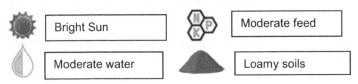

Mimusops elengi (Spanish Cherry)

Mimusops elengi is a evergreen tree, has fragrant flowers and edible fruit, often used in traditional medicine and ornamental purposes.

DISTRIBUTION

- Native
- Naturalised

It is native to India, Myanmar and Sri Lanka, Southeast Asia and Australia.

Mimusops elengi (Spanish Cherry)

SUMMARY

Common Name	Spanish cherry
Height	Up to 45 feet
Flower	White colour
Light	Bright sun
Origin	India, Southeast Asia, Australia
Scientific name	*Mimusops elengi*
Family	Sapotaceae

MEDICINAL WHEEL

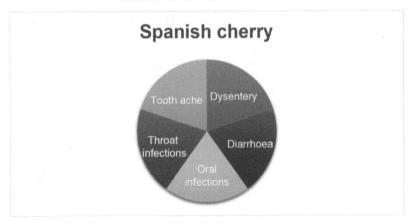

Also used to treat worm infestations and poisonous cases.

GROWING TIPS

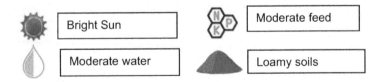

Murraya koenigii (Curry leaf)

The curry tree or *Murraya koenigii*, is a tropical and sub-tropical tree native to Asia.

DISTRIBUTION

- Native
- Naturalised

It is native to India and Indo China regions.

Murraya koenigii (Curry leaf)
SUMMARY

Common Name	Curry leaf /Karivepallai
Height	Up to 15 feet
Flower	White colour
Light	Bright Sun
Origin	India, Indo China
Scientific name	*Murraya koenigii*
Family	Rutaceae

MEDICINAL WHEEL

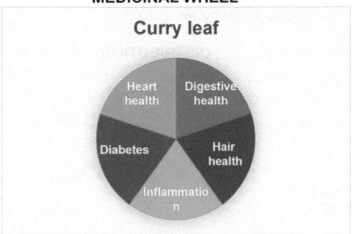

Curry leaf

Also used to improve immunity, bone and brain health, vision, piles, itching, fresh cuts.

GROWING TIPS

 Bright Sun

 Moderate feed

 Moderate water

 Loamy soils

Murraya paniculata (Orange jasmine)

Murraya paniculata commonly known as orange jasmine is a tropical, evergreen plant bearing small, white, scented flowers, which is grown as an ornamental tree or hedge.

DISTRIBUTION

■ Native
■ Naturalised

It is native to Southern China, Taiwan, India, Nepal, Northeastern Pakistan, Sri Lanka, Southeastern Asia and Northern Australia.

Murraya paniculata (Orange jasmine)

SUMMARY

Common Name	Orange Jasmine/ Mock Orange/ Mock Lime
Height	Up to 20 feet
Flower	White
Light	Bright Sun
Origin	South east Asia and Northern Australia
Scientific name	*Murraya paniculata*
Family	Rutaceae

MEDICINAL WHEEL

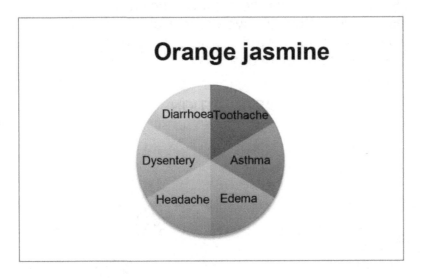

Also used to treat thrombosis, digestive disorders, cardiovascular disorders.

GROWING TIPS

 Bright Sun

 Moderate feed

 Moderate water

 Loamy soils

Mussaenda frondosa (Dhobi tree)

Mussaenda frondosa commonly known as the wild mussaenda or dhobi tree is a plant of family Rubiaceae.

DISTRIBUTION

■ Native
■ Naturalised

It is native to the Indian subcontinent and South East Asia.

Mussaenda frondosa (Dhobi tree)

SUMMARY

Common Name	Dhobi Tree / White flag bush
Height	Up to 6 feet
Flower	Red / orange colour with white
Light	Bright Sun, Semi shade
Origin	Indian subcontinent
Scientific name	*Mussaenda frondosa*
Family	Rubiaceae

MEDICINAL WHEEL

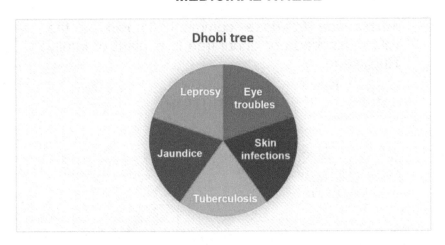

Also used to treat ulcers, wounds and bronchitis.

GROWING TIPS

  Bright Sun/ Semi shade   Moderate feed

 Moderate water   Loamy soils

Nelumbo nucifera (Lotus)

Nelumbo nucifera commonly called as sacred lotus is a perennial aquatic plant known for its large showy flowers and distinctive round leaves which float on the water surface.

DISTRIBUTION

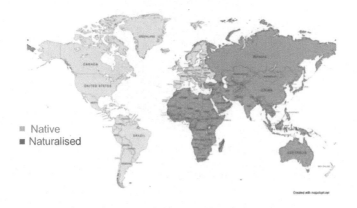

■ Native
■ Naturalised

It is native to Asia, Australia and Africa.

Nelumbo nucifera (Lotus)

SUMMARY

Common Name	Lotus
Height	Up to 6 feet tall
Flower	Pink
Light	Bright Sun
Origin	Asia, Australia, Africa
Scientific name	*Nelumbo nucifera*
Family	Nelumbonaceae

MEDICINAL WHEEL

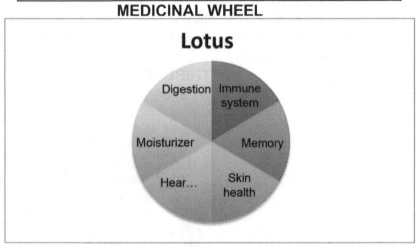

Also treats constipation and pain.

GROWING TIPS

Neolamarckia cadamba (Kadam)

Neolamarckia cadamba commonly known as kadam is commonly known for its large spherical cluster of fragrant flowers.

DISTRIBUTION

■ Native
■ Naturalised

It is native to India, Sri Lanka, Southern China, Indo China, Malaysia, Indonesia, Papua New Guinea.

Neolamarckia cadamba (Kadam)

SUMMARY

Common Name	Bur flower, Kadam
Height	Up to 90 feet
Flower	Orange, Yellow/ Golden
Light	Bright Sun
Origin	India, Indo China, Sri Lanka
Scientific name	*Neolamarckia cadamba*
Family	Rubiaceae

MEDICINAL WHEEL

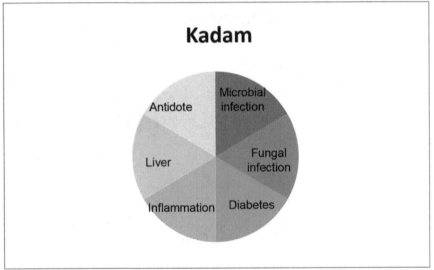

Also used to treat pains and tumuors.

GROWING TIPS

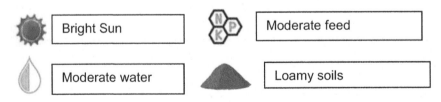

215

Nerium oleander (Oleander)

Nerium oleander is commonly known as oleander is a shrub or small tree in the family Apocynaceae.

DISTRIBUTION

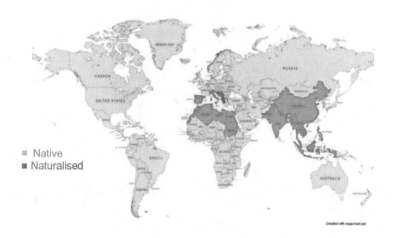

It is native to the Northern Africa, Southern Europe, Southeast Asia and to Indian subcontinent including India, Nepal, Pakistan and western China.

Nerium oleander (Oleander)

SUMMARY

Common Name	Oleander / Rosebay
Height	Up to 20 Feet
Flower	White / Red / Pink
Light	Bright Sun
Origin	Northern Africa, Southern Europe, Southeast Asia
Scientific name	*Nerium oleander*
Family	Apocynaceae

MEDICINAL WHEEL

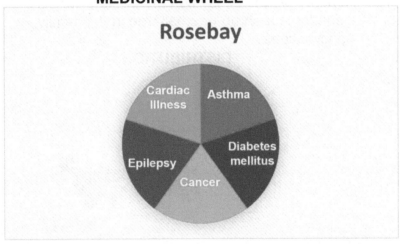

Also used in treatment of ulcers, leprosy, ringworm and scabies.

GROWING TIPS

 Bright Sun

 Moderate water

 Moderate feed

 Loamy soils

Nyctanthes arbortristis (Night jasmine)

Nyctanthes arbortristis is native to South Asia and Southeast Asia. It is commonly known as night-blooming jasmine, tree of sadness, tree of sorrow and coral jasmine.

DISTRIBUTION

It is native to India, Bangladesh, Nepal, Bhutan, Pakistan, Thailand and Sri Lanka.

Nyctanthes arbortristis (Night jasmine)

SUMMARY

Common Name	Night Blooming Jasmine
Height	Up to 30 Feet
Flower	White
Light	Bright Sun
Origin	Indian subcontinent
Scientific name	*Nyctanthes arbortristis*
Family	Oleaceae

MEDICINAL WHEEL

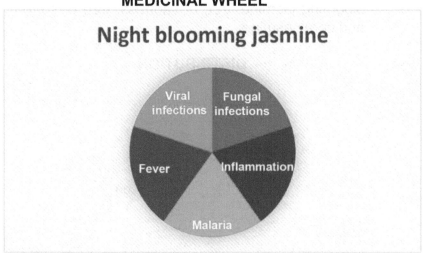

Also used to arthritis, lower back problems, stimulates immune system.

GROWING TIPS

 | Bright Sun | | Moderate feed |

 | Moderate water | | Loamy soils |

Nymphaea nouchali (Blue star water lily)

Nymphaea nouchali is a day blooming water lily with its roots and stems submerged within.

DISTRIBUTION

- Native
- Naturalised

It is native to south and east Asia.

Nymphaea nouchali (Blue star water lily)

SUMMARY

Common Name	Blue star water lily
Height	Up to 1 feet tall
Flower	Blue, Pink, White
Light	Bright Sun
Origin	Asia
Scientific name	*Nymphaea nouchali*
Family	Nymphaeaceae

MEDICINAL WHEEL

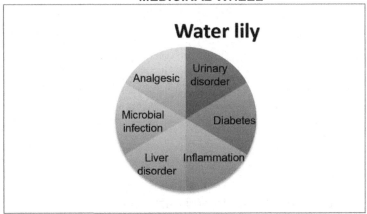

Also has richer antioxidants.

GROWING TIPS

 Bright Sun

 High water

 Moderate feed

 Loamy soils

Ocimum gratissimum (Clove Basil)

Ocimum gratissimum is a perennial herb in the family Lamiaceae.

DISTRIBUTION

■ Native
■ Naturalised

It is native to Tropical Africa, Madagascar, south east Asia and the Bismarck Archipelago. It is naturalised in Mexico, Panama, West Indies, Brazil and Bolivia.

Ocimum gratissimum (Clove Basil)

SUMMARY

Common Name	Clove Basil/ African Basil
Height	Up to 9 feet
Flower	White/ Green/ Dull white/ Pale yellow
Light	Bright sun
Origin	India , Tropical Africa and South East Asia
Scientific name	*Ocimum gratissimum*
Family	Lamiaceae

MEDICINAL WHEEL

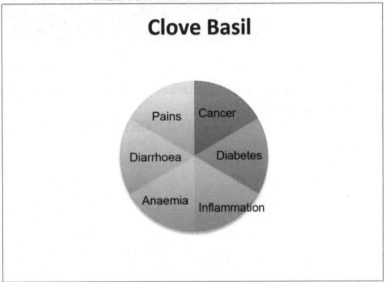

Also used to treat digestive disorders, kidney complaints, infections, tonsillitis.

GROWING TIPS

 Bright Sun

 Moderate feed

 Moderate water

 Loamy soils

Ocimum teuiflorum (Holy Basil)

Ocimum tenuiflorum commonly known as holy basil or tulsi is an aromatic perennial plant.

DISTRIBUTION

■ Native
■ Naturalised

It is native to Indian subcontinent and Southeast Asia.

Ocimum teuiflorum (Holy Basil)

SUMMARY

Common Name	Tulsi / Holy Basil
Height	Up to 1.8 feet
Flower	Pink and white colour
Light	Bright Sun
Origin	Indian subcontinent
Scientific name	*Ocimum tenuiflorum*
Family	Lamiaceae.

MEDICINAL WHEEL

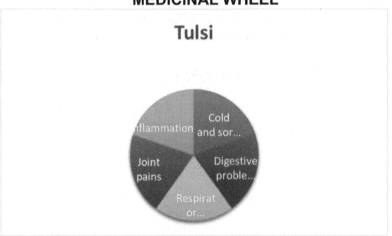

Also used to treat kidney stones, blood pressure, viral, fungal and bacterial infections.

GROWING TIPS

 Bright sun

 Low feed

 Moderate water

 Loamy soils

Orthosiphon aristatus (Cats whiskers)

Orthosiphon aristatus commonly known as cat's whiskers or Java tea is a shrub in the family Lamiaceae.

DISTRIBUTION

It is native to southern China, the Indian Subcontinent, South East Asia and Australia.

Orthosiphon aristatus (Cats whiskers)

SUMMARY

Common Name	Cats whiskers/ Java tea/ Kidneys tea plant
Height	Up to 3 feet
Flower	White
Light	Bright Sun
Origin	Tropical Asia
Scientific name	*Orthosiphon aristatus*
Family	Lamiaceae

MEDICINAL WHEEL

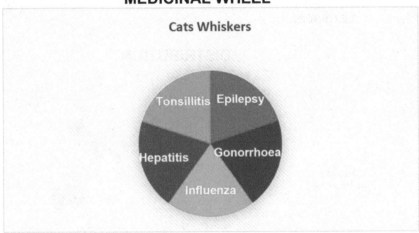

Also used to treat menstrual disorders, gallstones, abdominal pain, psoriasis.

GROWING TIPS

 Bright Sun

 Moderate feed

 Moderate water

 Loamy soils

Persicaria chinensis (Chinese knotweed)

Persicaria chinensis commonly known as creeping smartweed or Chinese knotweed is a plant species from the family Polygonaceae.

DISTRIBUTION

It is native to Indian subcontinent, Indo china, Philippines, Malaysia, Indonesia, China and Japan.

Persicaria chinensis (Chinese knotweed)

SUMMARY

Common Name	Chinese knotweed
Height	Up to 3 feet
Flower	White / Pink
Light	Bright Sun/ Semi shade
Origin	Indian subcontinent, Indochina, China, Japan
Scientific name	*Persicaria chinensis*
Family	Polygonaceae

MEDICINAL WHEEL

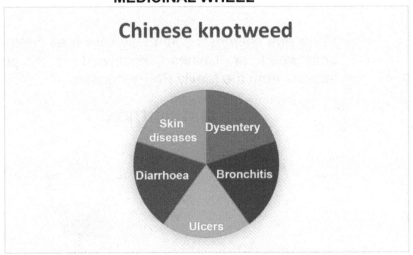

Also used to treat viral infections, skin diseases and sore throat.

GROWING TIPS

  Bright Sun/ Semi shade   Moderate feed

 High water   Loamy soils

Persicaria polygonum (Spotted ladysthumb)

Persicaria polygonum is in a genus of about 130 species of flowering plants in the buckwheat and knotweed family Polygonaceae.

DISTRIBUTION

It is native to North America. It is naturalised in India, Nepal, Sri Lanka, South China, Afghanistan, South Japan and Malaysia.

Persicaria polygonum (Spotted ladysthumb)

SUMMARY

Common Name	Spotted ladysthumb
Height	Up to 3.5 feet
Flower	White / Pink
Light	Bright Sun, Semi shade
Origin	North America
Scientific name	*Persicaria polygonum*
Family	Polygonaceae

MEDICINAL WHEEL

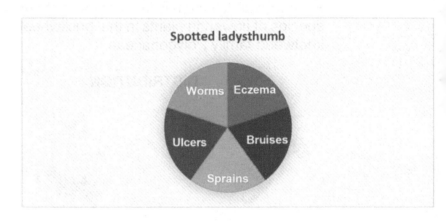

Spotted ladysthumb

It is used to treat gastrointestinal and neurological disorders, acts as an antidote for snake and scorpion bites.

GROWING TIPS

 Bright Sun/ Semi shade

 Moderate feed

 Moderate water

 Loamy soils

Phyllanthus emblica L. (Amla)

Phyllanthus emblica L. commonly known Indian gooseberry, Malacca tree or amla is a deciduous tree.

DISTRIBUTION

■ Native
■ Naturalised

Phyllanthus emblica is a deciduous tree, that is native to India and is grown in many countries like China, Malaysia, Bangladesh, Myanmar, Sri Lanka, Pakistan and Uzbekistan.

232

Phyllanthus emblica L. (Amla)

SUMMARY

Common Name	Indian Gooseberry / Amla
Height	Up to 25 feet
Flower	Greenish colour
Light	Bright Sun
Origin	Indian subcontinent
Scientific name	*Phyllanthus emblica* L.
Family	Phyllanthaceae

MEDICINAL WHEEL

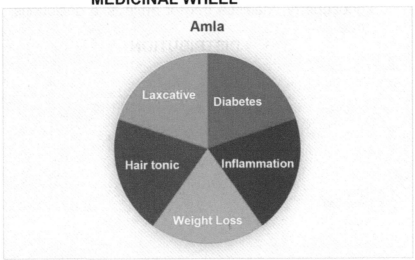

Also used to treat common cold, stomach infections, peptic ulcer.

GROWING TIPS

 Bright sun

 Moderate feed

 Moderate water

 Loamy soils

Piper betel (Betel vine)

Betel leaf is a climbing shrub known for its glossy heart shaped leaves.

DISTRIBUTION

It is native to Southeast Asia, including India, Phillipinnes, Indonesia, Indo China, Vietnam, Cambodia, Laos, Thailand, Myanmar, Timor Leste and Malaysia.

Piper betel (Betel vine)

SUMMARY

Common Name	Betel leaf
Height	Up to 12 feet
Flower	White
Light	Semi shade
Origin	Southeast Asia
Scientific name	*Piper betel*
Family	Piperaceae

MEDICINAL WHEEL

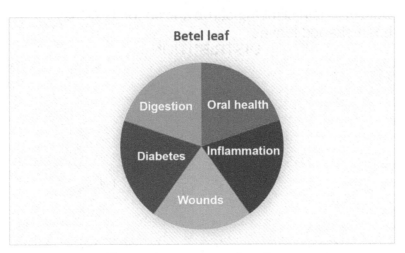

Also acts as an analgesic.

GROWING TIPS

 Semi shade

 Moderate feed

 High water

 Loamy soils

Piper longum (Long pepper)

Long pepper is commonly called Indian long pepper or pippali is a flowering vine in the family Piperaceae cultivated for its fruit which is usually dried and used as a spice and seasoning .

DISTRIBUTION

■ Native
■ Naturalised

It is native to India, Sri Lanka, Malaysia, Nepal, Vietnam.

Piper longum (Long pepper)

SUMMARY

Common Name	Pepper
Height	Up to 18 feet
Flower	Golden/ Yellow
Light	Semi shade
Origin	India
Scientific name	*Piper longum*
Family	Piperaceae

MEDICINAL WHEEL

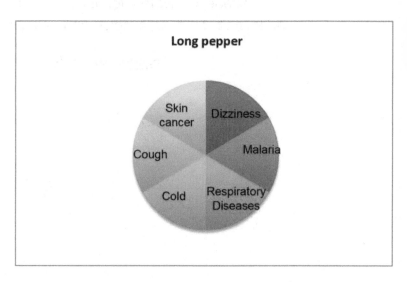

It is used to treat gastricitis, arthritis, asthma, nerve pain, scabies and vitiligo.

GROWING TIPS

 Semi shade   Moderate feed

 High water   Loamy soils

Plumbago auriculata (Cape plumbago)

Plumbago has clusters of pale blue flowers that blooms all around the year.

DISTRIBUTION

- Native
- Naturalised

The plant is native to South Africa and Mozambique and naturalised in India .

Plumbago auriculata (Cape plumbago)

SUMMARY

Common Name	Blue plumbago / cape plumbago / Forget- Me - Not
Height	Up to 3 feet
Flower	Blue
Light	Bright Sun
Origin	South Africa
Scientific name	*Plumbago auriculata*
Family	Plumbaginaceae

MEDICINAL WHEEL

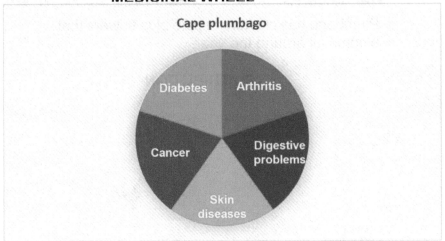

Cape plumbago

Also used to treat skin diseases, scabies, nervous system disorders.

GROWING TIPS

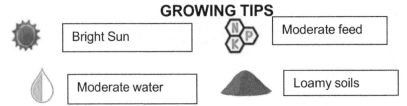

Bright Sun

Moderate feed

Moderate water

Loamy soils

Portulaca grandiflora (Table rose)

Portulaca grandiflora is a succulent annual or sub shrub flowering plant in the family Portulacaceae.

DISTRIBUTION

■ Native
■ Naturalised

It is native to southern Brazil, Argentina and Uruguay and is naturalised in India, Europe and parts of South America.

Portulaca grandiflora (Table rose)

SUMMARY

Common Name	Table rose / Mexican rose/ Moss rose
Height	Up to 1 feet
Flower	Orange / Pink / Red
Light	Bright Sun
Origin	Brazil , Argentina, Uruguay
Scientific name	*Portulaca grandiflora*
Family	Portulacaceae

MEDICINAL WHEEL

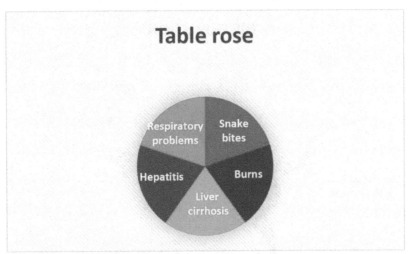

Table rose

Also used to treat pharyngeal oedema, eczema, insomnia

.GROWING TIPS

 Bright Sun Low feed

 Moderate water Loamy soils

Premna serratifolia (Headache tree)

Premna serratifolia is a species of small tree or shrub in the family Lamiaceae. It blooms and fruits between May and November. During flowering season, it attracts a large number of butterflies and bees.

DISTRIBUTION

■ Native
■ Naturalised

It is native to tropical and subtropical Asia, Eastern Africa and Western India

Premna serratifolia (Headache tree)

SUMMARY

Common Name	Headache Tree / Baus Baus
Height	Up to 30 feet
Flower	Green / White / Cream/ Off white
Light	Bright Sun/ Semi shade
Origin	Tropical Asia
Scientific name	*Premna serratiflora*
Family	Lamiaceae

MEDICINAL WHEEL

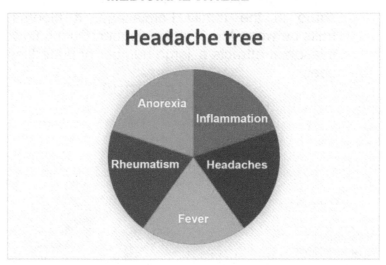

Also treats joint pains, cardiovascular diseases, arthritis, anorexia and jaundice.

GROWING TIPS

 Bright Sun/ Semi shade

 Moderate feed

 Moderate water

 Loamy soils

Psidium gujava (Guava)

Psidium guajava commonly known as guava is a tree that produces edible fruits rich in vitamin C and dietary fibre.

DISTRIBUTION

It is native to Tropical America, Mexico and Peru. It is naturalized in India, China, Thailand, Indonesia, Pakistan, Bangladesh, Philippines, Egypt, Kenya and Vietnam.

Psidium gujava (Guava)
SUMMARY

Common Name	Guava
Height	Up to 30 feet
Flower	White colour
Light	Bright Sun
Origin	Tropical America
Scientific name	*Psidium guajava*
Family	Myrtaceae

MEDICINAL WHEEL

It is used to treat gastroenteritis, menstrual disorders, lung and stomach cancers, hair health and blood pressure.

GROWING TIPS

 Bright Sun

 Moderate water

 Moderate feed

Loamy soils

Punica granatum (Pomegranate)

Punica granatum is commonly called as pomegranate is a fruit-bearing deciduous shrub in the family Lythraceae.

DISTRIBUTION

■ Native
■ Naturalised

It is native to Northern India, Iran, Pakistan, Afghanistan and Middle East.

Punica granatum (Pomegranate)
SUMMARY

Common Name	Pomegranate
Height	Up to 18 feet
Flower	Red, Yellow/ Golden
Light	Bright Sun, Semi shade
Origin	India, Iran and Afghanisthan
Scientific name	*Punica granatum*
Family	Lythraceae

MEDICINAL WHEEL

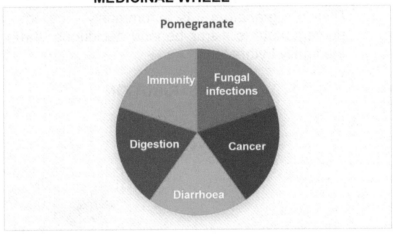

Also protects the heart, bacterial and fungal infections, pimples, rashes, improving memory and immunity.

GROWING TIPS

 Bright Sun/ Semi shade   Moderate feed

 Moderate water   Loamy soils

Rauvolfia tetraphylla (Sarpaganda)

Rauvolfia tetraphylla is a shrub in the family Apocynaceae known for its medicinal properties.

DISTRIBUTION

- Native
- Naturalised

It is native to Southeast Asia including India, Burma, Bangladesh, Sri Lanka and Malaysia.

248

Rauvolfia tetraphylla (Sarpaganda)

SUMMARY

Common Name	Sarpaganda/ Indian snakeroot
Height	Up to 1.5 Feet
Flower	White / Greenish white
Light	Bright Sun, Semi shade
Origin	Southeast Asia
Scientific name	*Rauvolfia tetraphylla*
Family	Apocynaceae

MEDICINAL WHEEL

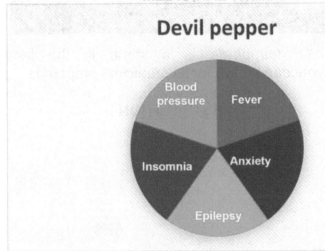

Devil pepper

Also used to treat hypertension, schizophrenia, cancer and brain diseases.

GROWING TIPS

 Bright Sun/ Semi shade

 Moderate feed

 Moderate water

 Loamy soils

Rhinacanthus nasutus (Snake Jasmine)

Rhinacanthus nasutus commonly known as snake jasmine is a shrub species native to tropical Asia.

DISTRIBUTION

It is native to Indochina (Cambodia, Laos, Myanmar, Vietnam), Southern China (Yunnan, Hainan, Guangdong), Malaysia, Indonesia, Philippines, Sri Lanka, India and Madagascar.

Rhinacanthus nasutus (Snake Jasmine)

SUMMARY

Common Name	Snake jasmine
Height	Up to 6 feet
Flower	White
Light	Bright Sun, Partial shade
Origin	Tropical Asia
Scientific name	*Rhinacanthus nasutus*
Family	Acanthaceae

MEDICINAL WHEEL

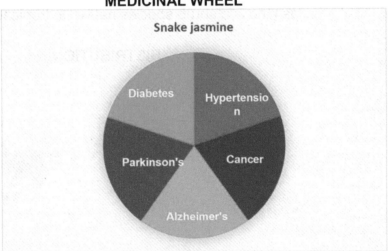

Also used to prevent dementia, poison bites,
ringworms, microbial infestations.

GROWING TIPS

 Bright Sun/ Semi shade

 Moderate feed

 Moderate water

 Loamy soils

Saccharum officinarum (Sugarcane)

Saccharum officinarum commonly known as sugarcane is a perennial grass. Sugarcane is a major source of sugar and ethanol.

DISTRIBUTION

■ Native
■ Naturalised

It is native to New Guinea. It is naturalized in India and Southeast Asia.

Saccharum officinarum (Sugarcane)

SUMMARY

Common Name	Sugarcane
Height	Up to 18 feet
Flower	Cream / Off-White, Pink, White
Light	Bright Sun
Origin	New Guinea
Scientific name	*Saccharum officinarum*
Family	Poaceae

MEDICINAL WHEEL

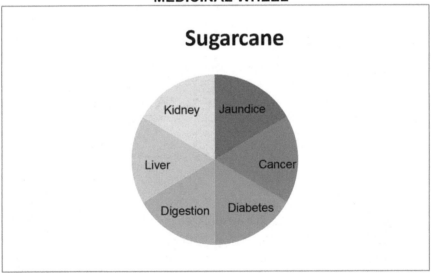

Also used to treat inflammations

GROWING TIPS

 Bright Sun

 High water

 Moderate feed

 Loamy soils

Salvia rosmarinus (Rosemary)

Salvia rosmarinus commonly known as rosemary is a shrub with fragrant, evergreen, needle-like leaves.

DISTRIBUTION

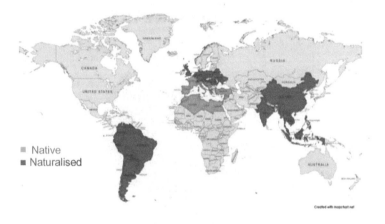

■ Native
■ Naturalised

It is native to Mediterranean region, Portugal and North western Spain. It is naturalised in Europe, South east Asia, China, south America.

Salvia rosmarinus (Rosemary)

SUMMARY

Common Name	Rosemary
Height	Up to 4 feet tall
Flower	White, pink, purple, Blue
Light	Bright Sun
Origin	Mediterranean
Scientific name	*Salvia rosmarinus*
Family	Lamiaceae

MEDICINAL WHEEL

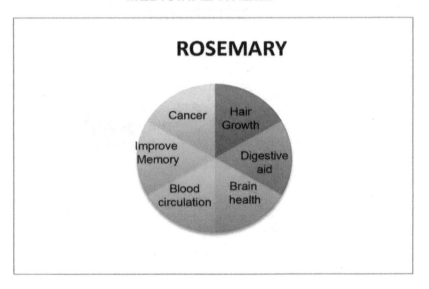

Also used in treating kidney and brain health.

GROWING TIPS

Sambucus nigra (Elder Berry)

Sambucus nigra is a species of flowering plant in the family Viburnaceae. Common names include elder, elderberry and black elder.

DISTRIBUTION

It is native to Europe and North America. It is naturalised in India.

Sambucus nigra (Elder Berry)

SUMMARY

Common Name	Elder Berry
Height	Up to 20 feet
Flower	White
Light	Bright Sun, Semi shade
Origin	Europe, North America
Scientific name	*Sambucus nigra*
Family	Viburnaceae

MEDICINAL WHEEL

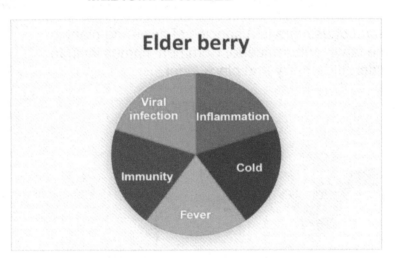

Also used to treat skin conditions, obesity, constipation, stress and cardiac disorders.

GROWING TIPS

 Bright Sun/ Semi shade

 Moderate feed

 High water

 Loamy soils

Sapindus mukorossi (Indian soapberry)

The soapnut tree is a deciduous tree containing a glucoside helps with its foaming properties.

DISTRIBUTION

It is native to India, Japan, China and Pakistan.

Sapindus mukorossi (Indian soapberry)

SUMMARY

Common Name	Indian soapberry
Height	Up to 60 feet tall
Flower	Greenish white colour
Light	Semi shade
Origin	India, Japan, China, Pakistan
Scientific name	*Sapindus mukorossi*
Family	Sapindaceae

MEDICINAL WHEEL

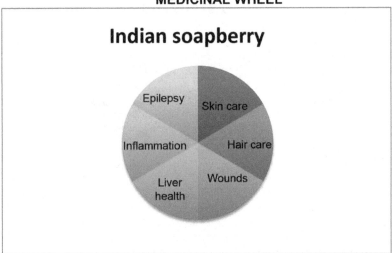

Also treats protozoal infections and migranes.

GROWING TIPS

 Semi shade

 Moderate feed

 Moderate water

 Loamy soils

Spilanthes acmella var. paniculata (Toothache plant)

Spilanthes acmella var. *paniculata* is commonly called Tooth ache plant is a perennial herbaceous plant cultivated throughout the year as ornamental or medicinal plant.

DISTRIBUTION

Native
Naturalised

It is native to Bangladesh, Indonesia, Nepal, Papua New Guinea, India, Sri Lanka, Thailand, Viet Nam, China, Brazil, Colombia, Ecuador, Peru and Taiwan.

Spilanthes acmella var. paniculata (Toothache plant)

SUMMARY

Common Name	Toothache Plant
Height	Up to 1 feet
Flower	Orange yellow
Light	Bright sun
Origin	Indian subcontinent, China
Scientific name	*Spilanthes acmella* var. *paniculata*
Family	Asteraceae

MEDICINAL WHEEL

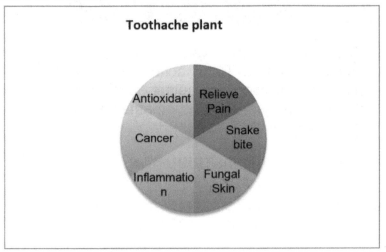

Also used to treat toothaches, stammering in children.

GROWING TIPS

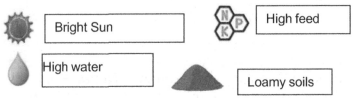

Bright Sun

High feed

High water

Loamy soils

Stachytarpheta jamaicensis (Blue snake weed)

Stachytarpheta jamaicensis is commonly known as Blue snake weed is a subshrub in the family Verbanaceae.

DISTRIBUTION

■ Native
■ Naturalised

It is native to Central and Southern America, Caribbean. It is naturalised in India, Africa and Mexico.

Stachytarpheta jamaicensis (Blue snake weed)

SUMMARY

Common Name	Blue snake weed /Brazilian tea/ Rooter comb
Height	Up to 3 feet
Flower	Blue / Purple
Light	Bright Sun, Semi shade
Origin	America, Caribbean
Scientific name	*Stachytarpheta jamaicensis*
Family	Verbenaceae

MEDICINAL WHEEL

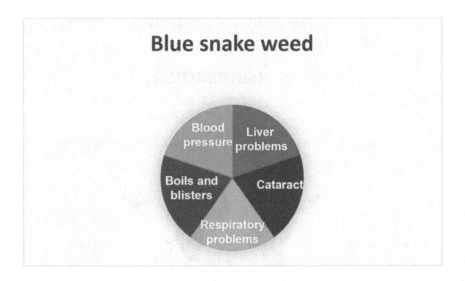

Also used to treat gastrointestinal tract problems, chills and fever, Hepatitis and Asthma .

GROWING TIPS

 Bright Sun/ Semi shade

 Moderate feed

 Moderate water

 Loamy soils

Strobilanthes alternata (Red flame ivy)

Strobilanthes alternata commonly known as Red Flame Ivy is a prostrate plant with attractive purple colored leaves.

DISTRIBUTION

■ Native
■ Naturalised

This plant is native to Malaysia and South East Asia. This natural herb grows in plenty across India, China, Indonesia and Japan.

Strobilanthes alternata (Red flame ivy)

SUMMARY

Common Name	Metal Leaf/ Red flame ivy
Height	Up to 1 feet
Flower	White
Light	Bright Sun, Semi shade
Origin	South-eastern Asia
Scientific name	*Strobilanthes alternata*
Family	Acanthaceae

MEDICINAL WHEEL

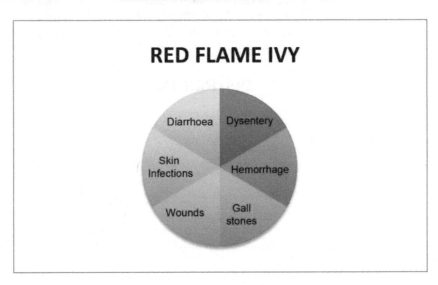

Also used to treat fresh cuts, to stop external bleeding.

GROWING TIPS

  Bright Sun/ Semi shade

 Moderate feed

 Moderate water

 Loamy soils

Strobilanthes hamiltoniana (Chinese Rainbell)

Strobilanthus hamiltoniana is commonly called as Chinese Rainbell is a soft stemmed evergreen shrub.

DISTRIBUTION

■ Native
■ Naturalised

It is native to India, Burma, Thailand , Nepal, Bangladesh, Bhutan, southern China, Taiwan, Laos and Vietnam.

Strobilanthus hamiltoniana (Chinese rainbell)

SUMMARY

Common Name	Chinese Rainbell
Height	Up to 6 feet
Flower	Purple
Light	Semi shade
Origin	Indian subcontinent
Scientific name	*Strobilanthus hamiltoniana*
Family	Acanthaceae

MEDICINAL WHEEL

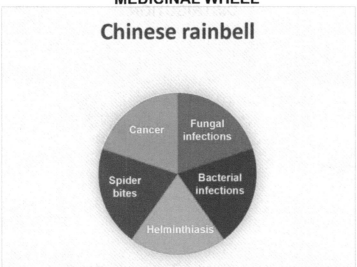

Also acts as a diuretic and is rich in antioxidants.

GROWING TIPS

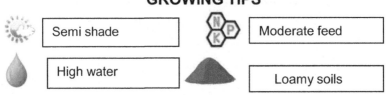

Semi shade		Moderate feed	
High water		Loamy soils	

Syzygium aromaticum (Clove)

Syzygium aromaticum commonly called as clove

is a tropical evergreen tree.

DISTRIBUTION

It is native to Indonesia. It is naturalized in Madagascar, Malaysia, Sri Lanka, India, Brazil and Tanzania.

Syzygium aromaticum (Clove)

SUMMARY

Common Name	Clove
Height	Up to 60 feet
Flower	Green, Pink, red, Crimson or Purple
Light	Bright sun
Origin	Indonesia
Scientific name	*Syzygium aromaticum*
Family	Myrtaceae

MEDICINAL WHEEL

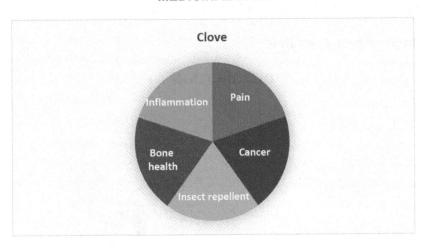

GROWING TIPS

 Bright Sun

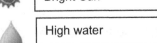 High water

 Moderate feed

 Loamy soils

Syzygium caryophyllatum (South Indian Plum)

Syzygium caryophyllatum is a small evergreen tree in the family Myrtaceae.

DISTRIBUTION

■ Native
■ Naturalised

It is native to Sri Lanka and south India.

Syzygium caryophyllatum (South Indian Plum)

SUMMARY

Common	South Indian Plum
Height	Up to 15 feet
Flower	White
Light	Bright Sun
Origin	India and Sri Lanka
Scientific name	*Syzygium caryophyllatum*
Family	Myrtaceae

MEDICINAL WHEEL

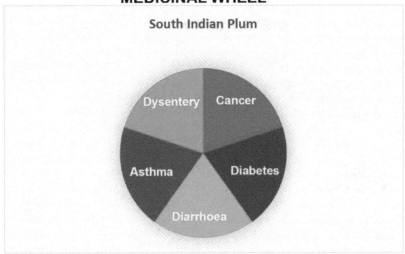

South Indian Plum

Also used to treat stomatitis, sore throat, microbial infections.

GROWING TIPS

Bright Sun/ Semi shade

Moderate feed

Moderate water

Loamy soils

Tabernamontana divaricata (Crepe jasmine)

Tabernaemontana divaricata is a shrub known for its white flowers and dark green glossy leaves.

\

DISTRIBUTION

■ Native
■ Naturalised

It is native to India, Bangladesh, south and central China, Nepal, Cambodia, Loas, Mynmar, Thailand and Vietnam.

Tabernamontana divaricata (Crepe jasmine)

SUMMARY

Common Name	Pinwheel flower, Crepe jasmine, Coffee rose
Height	Up to 6 feet tall
Flower	White
Light	Bright Sun/ Semi shade
Origin	India, Southeast Asia, Nepal and Bangladesh
Scientific name	*Tabernaemontana divaricata*
Family	Apocynaceae

MEDICINAL WHEEL

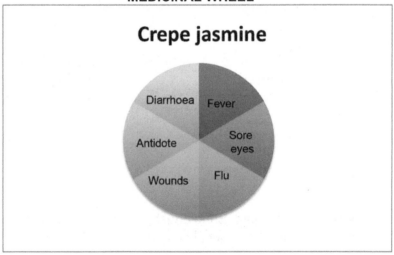

GROWING TIPS

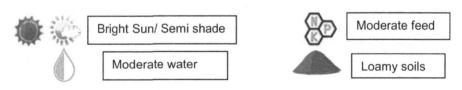

Bright Sun/ Semi shade

Moderate water

Moderate feed

Loamy soils

273

Trigonella foenum-graecum (Fenugreek)

Methi is the Indian name for Fenugreek. It is known for its culinary and medicinal uses as seeds and leaves being used in various dishes and traditional medicine.

DISTRIBUTION

■ Native
■ Naturalised

It is native to Western Asia, India, Argentina, Egypt and United States.

Trigonella foenum-graecum (Fenugreek)

SUMMARY

Common Name	Fenugreek / Methi
Height	Up to 0.7 feet
Flower	White to Yellow colour
Light	Bright sun/ Semi shade
Origin	Western Asia, Mediterranean region
Scientific name	*Trigonella foenum-graecum*
Family	Fabaceae

MEDICINAL WHEEL

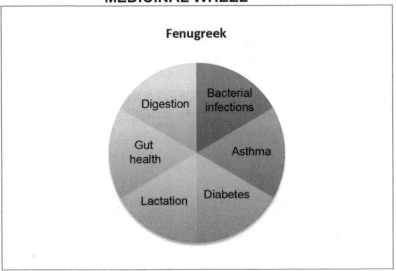

Also used to treat gut health, bacterial and fungal infections.

GROWING TIPS

 Bright sun

 Low feed

 Moderate water

 Loamy soils

Vitex negundo (Chinese chastetree)

Vitex negundo commonly known as Five Leaf Chaste Tree is a tree in the family Lamiaceae.

DISTRIBUTION

■ Native
■ Naturalised

It is native to Eastern and southern Africa, tropical and subtropical Asia.

Vitex negundo (Chinese chastetree)

SUMMARY

Common Name	Five Leaf Chaste tree/ Lagundi/ Nirgundi
Height	Up to 25 feet
Flower	Blue
Light	Bright Sun
Origin	Africa and Asia
Scientific name	*Vitex negundo*
Family	Lamiaceae

MEDICINAL USES

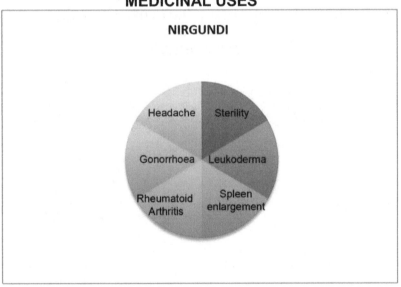

Also used to treat filarial diseases, bronchitis.

GROWING TIPS

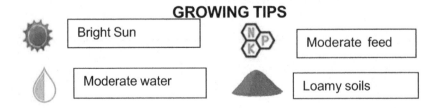

Bright Sun

Moderate feed

Moderate water

Loamy soils

Withania somnifera Dunal (Ashwaganda)

Withania somnifera Dunal commonly called as Ashwagandha or winter cherry is an evergreen shrub. The flowers are small, green and bell-shaped while ripe fruit is orange-red.

DISTRIBUTION

■ Native
■ Naturalised

Withania somnifera Dunal is native to India, Middle East and South Africa.

Withania somnifera Dunal (Ashwaganda)

SUMMARY

Common name	Ashwagandha
Height	Up to 3 feet tall
Flower colour	Greenish-yellow
Light	Bright Sun
Origin	India , Middle East &South Africa
Scientific name	*Withania somnifera* Dunal
Family	Solanaceae

MEDICINAL WHEEL

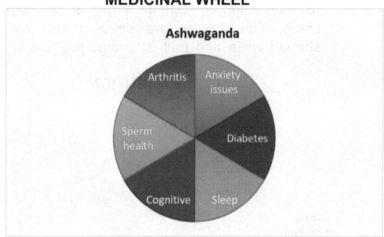

Also treats diabetes and arthritis.

GROWING TIPS

Bright Sun/ Semi shade

Low feed

Moderate water

Sandy loam/ loamy

Zingiber zerumbet (Shampoo ginger)

Zingiber zerumbet is a perennial plant known for its rhizotamous growth and striking pinecone like inflorescences.

DISTRIBUTION

■ Native
■ Naturalised

It is native to tropical Asia and Australia.

Zingiber zerumbet (Shampoo ginger)

SUMMARY

Common name	Shampoo ginger/ Pinecone ginger
Height	Up to 4 feet tall
Flower colour	Red
Light	Semi shade
Origin	Asia and Australia
Scientific name	*Zingiber zerumbet*
Family	Zingiberaceae

MEDICINAL WHEEL

Shampoo ginger

Cough · Skin irritation · Hair care · Fever · Stomach issues · Pain relief

Also cures diarrhoea, dysentery and prevents cancer.

GROWING TIPS

 Semi shade

 Moderate feed

 High water

 Loamy soils

INDEX

SOURCE CREDITS AND ACKNOWLEGEMENTS

1. Pixabay for some of the pictures of the species listed.
2. Freepik for some of the pictures of the species listed and the growing tips.
3. Adobe free pics for some of the pictures of species listed.
4. Map chart for the maps used.
5. Wikipedia for aiding our research.
6. Vikas bhat photos of species and images for the front and back cover.
   Front cover: *Orthosiphon aristatus* (Cats whiskers)
   Back cover: *Asystasia gangetica* (Chinese violet)
7. Mr. Sanjay Balu , Dr. Varsha Balu & Dr. Poorvi Bhat for valuable inputs.
8. Ms. Srushti Venkatesh and Mr. Sandeep Rawal for their help in production of the book.

ABOUT THE AUTHORS

Vikas Bhat is a natural farmer with over 40 years of experience. His expertise spans from farming of commercial crops, ayurvedic herbs and organic animal husbandry

After being inspired by Fukuoka he began his career with organic farming, he has experience growing 500 medicinal herbs and plants. He is personally involved in rewilding over 1000 acres in Southern India. He founded Asia's first certified organic dairy farm in 2005

He has expertise in farming in several geo-climatic zones and specialises in reforestation of disrupted lands

His interest moved to smaller non-charismatic plants after noticing a lacunae in accessible information about them

He spends his free time documenting plant communities in their natural habitats and continues to discover new species. He has rediscovered one endemic genus (Karnataka) which was believed to be extinct for the last 175 years

He has made significant contributions to the field of nature education through his videos, where he talks about plant communities and helps educate people about the importance of preserving our natural resources

He is currently the chairman of MN Biodiversity and Rewilding Projects, whose aim is to bring native plants back into landscaping, providing these plants a second chance at survival in your garden and making every customer a conservationist.

www.khandigeorganic.com

www.rewildiversity.com

MN BIODIVERSITY
—— REWILDING PROJECTS ——

Vivek Balu has extensive experience as a wildlife enthusiast and environmentalist. His passion for birdwatching not only enhances his understanding of avian species but also plays a crucial role in raising awareness about biodiversity and the need for protection of natural habitats. He was closely involved in rewilding of 50+ acres bordering a national park in Southern India.

His long-term involvement in these areas allows him to make significant contributions to conservation efforts, whether through research, education, or community engagement.

Vivek Balu's active involvement in rewilding projects in Southern India, along with his extensive travels, speaks volumes about his dedication to environmental conservation. His passion for writing about native species is a wonderful way to spread awareness and educate others about their importance.

Vivek Balu's role as Managing Director & CEO of MN Biodiversity & Rewilding Projects, combined with his entrepreneurial background, gives him a unique perspective on integrating business and environmental sustainability.

www.rewildiversity.com

MN BIODIVERSITY
—— REWILDING PROJECTS ——

Appendix: Feedback/ Appreciation

DEPARTMENT OF BOTANY
CATHOLICATE COLLEGE, PATHANAMTHITTA
Basil Hills, Makkamkunnu P. O., 689 645, Kerala, India
(Affiliated to M.G.University, Kottayam, Kerala, NAAC Reaccredited with A+ Grade)

Dr. THOMAS V. P., Ph.D.
Assistant Professor
Principal Investigator, Major Project
KSCSTE 29/SRLS/2014

APPRECIATION LETTER

Dear Mr. Vikas Bhat,

I hope this letter finds you well. I am writing to express our sincere gratitude for your exceptional support and guidance in our Plant Taxonomy research.

Your mentorship has been invaluable to our PhD scholars, particularly during their fieldwork. Your extensive knowledge and expertise have significantly contributed to the depth and quality of our research.

We are deeply inspired by your passion for nature and your dedication to educating others about its importance. Your efforts to share your knowledge through social media have not only enlightened us but also reached a wider audience, fostering a greater appreciation for the natural world.

We are immensely grateful for the time and effort you have dedicated to our research. Your support has been a cornerstone of our research, and we are truly grateful for your commitment and enthusiasm.

With warm regards,

Dr. Thomas V.P.

Tel : 0468 - 2222223 (Office), 9496362917 (Mob.), E-mail : amomum@gmail.com

1

292